YOUNG VERMONTERS

YOUNG VERMONTERS

Not an Endangered Species

Joe Sherman & Martina Tesařová

BLACK FALLS PRESS
Montgomery, Vermont

Designed and composed at Hobblebush Books, Brookline, New Hampshire (www.hobblebush.com)

Printed in the United States of America

ISBN 978-0-9830687-2-3
Library of Congress Control Number: 2010915720

Published by:

BLACK FALLS PRESS
P.O. Box 102
Montgomery, Vermont 05470

For
Young Vermonters
Everywhere

Contents

A Self-Interview as Preface

Joe Sherman / Self Interview

What's this book about?

It's my response to the claim that young Vermonters can't live in Vermont anymore. I wanted to challenge the conviction that it's too expensive for them, they can't find jobs, that they can't make it here.

Why did you decide to do interviews instead of writing a conventional book?

Interviews aren't exactly unconventional, but they're more raw, of the moment, capture a person in a different way. I really wanted that rawness, the one-off quality that interviews do best. I wanted the young Vermonters to speak for themselves.

The project really started out as something entirely different. I planned to do an update of *Fast Lane on a Dirt Road,* my contemporary history of Vermont. It wasn't contemporary anymore; the last update was in 2000. I thought I'd talk to some young Vermonters in their twenties and thirties about their lives in our times. I'd cherry pick the good parts, mix in a little broader history for context, and update my old book.

But it didn't work out that way. Right off, after a couple interviews, I had a problem. The interviews were richer, funnier, and sadder than I ever imagined. I reluctantly use the overused word *inspiring*, but that's what they were—they were great. They deserved a book of their own.

How did you pick the twenty people?

I'm not a very systematic person. I just asked my friends for help. I wanted a variety of people, so I asked a variety of friends for leads. It all worked organically, which was reassuring. Slowly, this sort of vine-like net emerged from the process and it gradually netted most of the state, from Brattleboro to Franklin. I'm pretty happy about that; I think I have a decent cross section of what a demographer might call my "target population."

Could you tell us a little about the young Vermonters in the book?

I'd rather not. I don't want to spoil the interviews for you. I will tell you there are ten men and ten women between the ages of twenty-one and thirty-eight. Two had just started new businesses, three were into the local-food movement. There are two musicians. There's a trial lawyer, an Abenaki chief's granddaughter, a blue-collar renegade who teaches people how to shoot a rifle and has a small arsenal of his own, a black man profiled in Burlington since he was twelve, a poster girl for foster care (she survived five high schools in four years in Vermont), a junior developer who saw the twin Trade Towers collapse. And so on.

And I only knew one of them beforehand. His grandfather appeared in *Fast Lane on a Dirt Road*. Two more I knew because I stay connected with their families. A fourth I had in an English class years ago. But sixteen of them I'd never laid eyes on before.

What kinds of questions did you ask them?

I kept it pretty simple and asked everyone the same things. Basically, I broke the questions into three categories: the past, the present, the future. I asked what I called my "classic Vermont questions": You ever milk a cow, tap a maple tree, hunt, fish, can food? I asked about cultural stuff. I regret not asking them if they ate pie for breakfast (a true Vermonter eats pie for breakfast-or at least he/she used to). I didn't ask everybody if they went to church either; I wish I'd done that.

I pre-interviewed everybody on the phone or by email, so I knew a little about them—but not too much. I wanted each actual interview to be fresh, to allow for surprises and chance. It worked surprisingly well. You talk to somebody for over an hour straight about themselves and you enter some interesting terrain. I'm sixty-five but I get along pretty well with younger people. I'm really bothered by the artificial barriers I think our culture and commerce often put between people of different age groups. I think it's destructive and unnatural. I really see us all in the same boat these days, sort of a leaky boat under threatening skies.

What about the subtitle, Not An Endangered Species? *What's that all about?*

A popular misconception is that young Vermonters can't survive here any more. They can't find jobs, can't buy a house. I didn't think that was true, but I'd been out of America much of the last decade (in Prague and smaller cities in central Europe), and once I started the interviews, I wanted to hear more about how they were doing.

The young Vermonters in these pages are not leaving the state. They're staying or have returned from away; they find living here tough but doable. But the whole issue needs more research and a longer perspective. One truth is that it's never been easy to live in Vermont (too rocky, too cold, too small, too backward, too liberal, too conservative), unless you were rich—and maybe not even then. That it's hard to stay here is part of the state's romantic allure. And the young have been leaving forever. After the Civil War there was an exodus, much of it to Wisconsin, where the land was flat and the soil deeper. During the 1950s, when I was a boy, Vermont farms were dying like flies on a November windowsill and anybody with half a brain and a bus ticket was often out of here. The sale of farms is what fed the real estate hunger that swept through the state with the ski-area boom. The back-to-the-land, naked-in-the-moonlight, roll-me-another-one crowd of the 1960s and 1970s, among which I returned, was an aberration. Sure, the population jumped 15 percent in the seventies and another 10 percent in the eighties, but since then the numbers have trended downward; population growth during the first decade of the new millennium is estimated around 3 percent.

The challenges young Vermonters face today to stay here, as I learned, are different from those in the past. But the times are tough everywhere now. They're also scary, a feeling often repeated in the interviews. So why not at least make a stand in a place you care for and love and feel part of? A theme connecting many of the interviews is the looming uncertainty of the future. To get through it, I heard, you'd be smart to find a community, make yourself part of it, get a life started that can last and make sense. Become sort of starter yeast for a saner planet.

Were there some things you didn't like about these young people, or any surprises?

Sure. It's like one of them, a preacher, said about his congregation: they're good people but not perfect; they're all too human. As individuals the young Vermonters I talked to were boastful, proud, judgmental, given to outbursts and displays of ego. Some have it really together, others are working on their vision of a future they haven't quite pulled off yet. But my photographer identified their collective specialness; she called it "unspoiled spirit." They were also resourceful, practical, optimistic in a restrained, realistic way. This varied mix of attributes gives them character. A uniquely Vermont character, I believe. A character that much of America, sad to say, seems to be in the long, slow, painful process of losing.

Surprises? Too much violence in some of their lives for one. Worry about returning veterans from Iraq and Afghanistan having a hard time readjusting. A distaste for country music, extensive use of social media but often with misgivings about what technology is doing to them as human beings. I was disturbed by the lack of knowledge of Vermont history that most of them—not all, but most—revealed to me. I wanted to remind them of George Santayana's famous quote, "Those who cannot remember the past are condemned to repeat it," and suggest they put it over their beds or work stations or on their Facebook pages.

The biggest surprise for me, though, was how much I learned from these young people. And how easily we talked. Sometimes I felt like we were in an endless verbal jazz jam. I loved that. I'll never forget it.

Final question. Are they all "true Vermonters"? Were they born and raised here?

No. Hard-core traditionalists probably won't be happy with me for including some young folks born outside of Vermont. But I'm pretty convinced it's time for the "Am I a Vermonter" question to be re-examined. Sure, being a multi-generational Vermonter has its own power. But newcomers have been so influential in the state for the last fifty years that to say you're not a Vermonter unless your grandpa is buried nearby and you eat apple pie for breakfast—I once sort of adhered to that definition, but not anymore. You know, I wasn't born here myself. I was born in Lebanon, New Hampshire, adopted by a mill-town family from Quechee. They took me home when I was ten days old. What does that make me? I have never quite figured that one out.

The interview questions

The present:

- *Do you think we're living in a dark economic era?*
- *What about your work? Could you describe it for me?*
- *Are there opportunities for you?*
- *What pisses you off, really makes you angry?*
- *Who makes up your community? Who do you trust?*
- *Are you a political person?*
- *At your core, are you more of a physical, emotional, or intellectual person?*

The past:

- *Are you a Vermont history buff?*
- *Where were you in 2000, when the decade began? What were you doing?*
- *Over the last decade, what was your high point? Your low point?*
- *If there was something you could change about the last ten years, what would it be?*
- *Could you give me a brief executive summary of your life over the last decade?*

The future:

- *Are you concerned about the future? What are you worried about?*
- *What is your vision of the next five, ten years, for you? For Vermont?*

The classic Vermont questions:

- *You ever milk a cow?*
- *Ever tap maple trees or make syrup?*
- *Do you can, or put food by?*
- *Do you hunt or fish?*
- *You do any winter sports?*

Cultural questions:

- *Do you use social media? Personally or professionally?*
- *Go to church? (Forewarning: I didn't ask this as often as I wish I had.)*
- *Do you read, listen to music, watch movies?*
- *Do you have a favorite quote?*

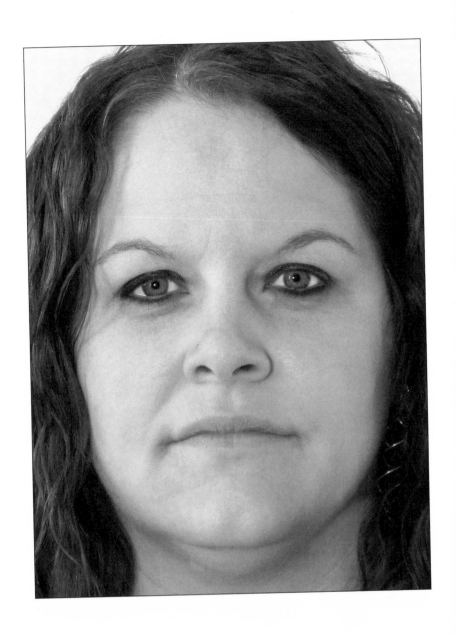

Accentuate the positive

Stacy Ashley

Born: December 1, 1971
Where: Randolph, VT
Siblings: One sister, older; one brother, younger
Married: Divorced, two kids
Job: Waitress

I meet Stacy in Sharon and follow her north on Route 14, past Dixie's
Diner where she works, and alongside the White River and through
South Royalton, heading up into the hills on a dirt road. We climb past
small farms, a few new homes, a number of shacks with trucks and
debris in the yards. The steep hills and windy road remind me we're
near my sister's old farm just across the Tunbridge town line. We're in a
last redoubt of not-so-well off Vermonters. On a hilltop Stacy turns up
a short dirt drive and we park at an old hunting camp where she lives
with her two kids, her mom and dad, and some dogs, all of which start
barking. Inside the camp, which the family is rebuilding into a house, are
Stacy's teenage son and daughter. Hunting trophies hang on the walls.
We sit at the kitchen table to talk.

Can you tell me a little about your job at Dixie's?

I waitress. I'm the only waitress there. Monday, Tuesday, and Wednesday
I work twenty-four hours for the three days. Thursday I work thirteen
hours. Saturday I work thirteen hours. I like it. A lot of older guys will
come and sit at the bar in the morning, drink coffee. That's pretty much
what they have is coffee. You hear a lot of tales from the olden days.

Do they talk politics?

They do talk politics. I don't get involved. Two things that you don't do
is talk politics nor tell them anything personal about yourself.

You tired at the end of a shift?

Not after eight hours, but when I do thirteen, yeah. I don't sit down at
all. I don't even sit to eat. I eat standing up, because people are in there
all the time.

You're the show.

I am.

The tips decent?

Yup. That's the only reason I'm there. [Before that] I ran my own day-care in New York for eight years in Ellenburg Depot. It's just outside Plattsburgh.

Why'd you come back to Vermont?

I lived with a gentleman for ten years out there, and three years ago his brother was murdered in Mooers, New York. I ended up coming back here because he was pretty devastated, my boyfriend. He really took it badly. I just got out. He retreated to drugs and alcohol. I had my two kids and didn't want to go through that.

What happened—his brother got shot?

A Canadian came across the border and shot him. Left him there and stole his truck and went all the way to Texas. They caught him going into Mexico. It was just random. They caught the guy. He went to prison.

So that sort of turned your life dark?

(Stacy nods.) Yeah. Before that, my boyfriend was a good guy. Before we ended up not liking him anymore, I just decided to leave.

Now we're in tough times economically and still in two wars. Do you feel that we're living in a tough era?

Yeah, yeah, I do. I've noticed just since I started working at Dixie's two years ago that we have gotten slow . . . slower definitely. People are afraid to spend. They're just holding on to what they have, you know. With gas prices and heating oil prices, I think people are scared.

Do you see that in your friends?

Yeah. A number of people here are not that well off. They live very simple. And I'm kind of a very simple-living person too. Raising two kids and being a single parent, I have to be very simple. I budget to get through the month. I give myself so much for gas money, for spending money. And I put a lot of money away.

(I glance around at the rifles, deer trophies, and stacked building materials.) Now, you said this was your dad's hunting camp?

He's living here with me and my mom. They're at work. They work at Thermal Dynamics [in West Lebanon, NH]. Thermal Dynamics slowed down for a while, but they're back to where it's normal. My mom has been there for thirty . . . almost thirty years. My dad has been there for five.

(Stacy thinks a moment.) I think we're going to have a hard time pulling out of what we're in. I watch the news all the time, I read the newspaper. We're definitely spending a lot of money out there that we don't have. Now we have this health care reform, yeah . . . .

Are there many opportunities for people around here?

Not a lot. In order to get a job, you have to travel. Pretty much around here you've got waitresses, store clerks. People go to Lebanon . . . Rutland. I have relatives who drive all the way to Burlington. It's where my dad worked before he started working for Thermal Dynamics.

All our small factories like Vermont Castings, they're all closing. They shut down. I think they didn't have it, the money, you know. Then they reopened, but with very few employees; the outdoor wood stoves are taking over the business.

What makes you mad? Does anything really get you angry?

You know what, I'm a very easy-going person. As long as people don't bother me, I don't bother them. I don't get mad very easily.

Who makes up your community? Who do you trust?

Umm . . . my sister—I have a sister—and her husband and my nephew. My brother, his wife. I have a few friends, but I work all the time, so I really don't get to go out much.

Are your family all good-natured, positive-thinking people?

Yeah. But the Iraq war has definitely changed my brother to a very hardcore person in many many ways. He's a good guy. It's just that fun-loving teddy bear that he used to be, he's not like that anymore. He's seen too much. I worry about him.

Actually, today, I just got two cards from him. He's tired of it. He's ready to come home. This is like his fifth tour over there.

Do you consider yourself an emotional, physical, or intellectual person?

I'm not emotional. Not really. I'm pretty independent. I do think a lot about things. About everything. A lot about my kids. Yup. Pretty much they're my entire world. I've been a single mom since they were four and six. I pretty much raised them on my own.

How about Vermont history? Are you much interested in that?

I'm interested in the old history because a lot of my family has been around here for many, many, many years. Some of them were the very first people here. At family gatherings there's a lot of talking. A lot of BS-ing and catching up. Sometimes you don't see them until those family gatherings, and pretty much, I'll tell you, Tunbridge Fair is one of the biggest times that we have the family gathering.

Over the last ten years was there a high point, a best time for you?

The best time for me . . . I gotta say it's now. My daughter's heading off

to college, you know. It's one of the last times I'm going to see her do a lot of things in high school. When you have small kids, you're pretty limited with what you can do. Now they're older, I can do things with them, like kayaking. And, you know, we went to Maine last year.

How about your low point?

I think the lowest point that I've ever been was going through two or three years ago. I lost a whole complete family out of that. [The shooting] left two young sons fatherless. I think that was the lowest I've ever been in my whole entire life. Your world was ripped upside down, and torn apart, all in a matter of just one second.

Can you summarize your last ten years briefly?

My last decade (Stacy says quietly, almost to herself), it's been interesting, sad, devastating at points. I'm amazed how I came out of it, and my children. We've gone through some turmoil.

Do you think it's made you in some way a tighter family?

Absolutely . . . sorry, I'm going to cry . . . it's definitely made us stronger. And we appreciate a lot more and our family's very important; you know, sometimes you seem to slack off but since that ordeal, our family's very important. You never know when somebody's going to be gone.

What are your concerns about the future?

I'm just concerned that it's easy for my daughter. I don't want her to struggle. You know, they're on their own. You hope you've instilled enough in them that they can make right choices and do good for themselves. I think my major concern right now is where they're headed and how is it going to turn out for them.

I do worry about my job cause you never know. I got that job when I went to breakfast with my mom one morning, after I moved here, jobless. I got the job that day. That was on Wednesday, and the following Saturday I started to work and I've been there ever since. It just all kind of fell into place. The money is good there because you're getting cash, and on top of that you've got a paycheck. But I do worry about it, especially sometimes when it's slow and you're like, Ohh, what am I going to do if I don't have this?

If it was just me, I wouldn't worry. But I have two kids, so you think, Where is it going to come from? It's overwhelming sometimes.

Are you interested in politics?

No.

Are there any political issues that fire up the guys who drink coffee at Dixie's every morning?

What gets them fired up is that there's not going to be anything for their children or their grandchildren. They think that they're going to be in debt; they're not going to have what we have. It's true. There's not going to be anything left over for them with Social Security and stuff when they get older. They like the governor [Jim Douglas]. They don't like the president. I won't even say what they say there. Yeah, you hear a lot about the president.

What would you like to see happen in your life over the five or so years?

Well, I really want to go back and finish nursing. I started out [with night classes at the Vocational Center at Hartford, Vermont], and then I ended up having my daughter, so I put myself aside. I love my job–don't get me wrong—but I don't foresee myself doing it for the rest of my life. But now I'd really like to return to nursing school. I'd like to do it within the next two years, believe it or not. I'm paying on a car for my daughter, I pay on my van. Once they're paid off, in a year, I hope to get back to school, starting off online. I checked into it. If I do it online, they say it'll take about six years. So I'd be in my late forties.

What do you like about nursing?

I like taking care of people. Even when I did daycare, I had to take care of kids.

Did you ever consider having your daycare here?

Yeah, but it's not a good economy for it. And especially, the area here . . . people would have to travel with their kids way up here.

Boondocks daycare.

(Stacy laughs.) Yeah.

I'm going to ask you some classic Vermont questions: You ever milked a cow?

Yup. My uncle's.

Do you make maple syrup?

No, we don't, but we used to. Their dad (nods at her son and daughter sitting nearby and listening to us), when we lived here years and years and years ago, his father had a sugar house. We helped him with it. It was right up here in Royalton.

How about putting food by, canning?

I can. We have a garden. We put up tomatoes. I don't do my own apples, but I go to the apple orchard and pick them and do apple sauce. Pickles. We put the food out in our storage shed. It's right out there. (Stacy points out a window.) It's a thing that my dad built. I don't know what it was before but it stays cold, even in the summer time.

Do you hunt?

I do hunt. The first time I shot a deer I was fifteen. We used to take a whole group of us, and we'd drive deer to us. It just happened to be that the deer was driven to me, and I shot it. I didn't get deer fever! The rifle's still hangin' around here somewhere.

What about fishing?

I fish all over. We have a bridge down here on Mill Road that we go to, and we have Spaldings bridge. We catch brook trout and a lot of suckers. (She gestures at a trophy salmon on a wall.) I caught that in Pulaski, New York, from a river bank. That was a good fishing trip.

You do any winter sports?

We do downhill skiing. This year we went to Bolton Valley.

I have a few cultural questions. Do you read books, listen to music, watch movies?

I do. I do it all. I like to read a lot of the older books. Let's see, the last book that I read . . . (she glances at her son.) What was the name of it, CJ? It's about a kid whose father and him took off and they actually lived in a wilderness.

("Alabama Moon," CJ speaks up.)

I liked that. I like a lot of true stories.

What do you like for music?

Country. I like the new country, but I like the old country too. And I like the old Bob Marley, I like reggae.

Do you like to dance?

(She smiles.) Yeah.

When's the last time you went dancing?

A long time ago. Tunbridge is having these shindigs up there [in a dance hall], but I haven't been. Between working and focusing on their sports and their school things, I'm busy.

Do you use social media much? Do you use Facebook?

Nope.

Do your kids use it?

Yup, but I don't. It's too high speed for me. The world has to slow down a little. Too much Internet, cell phones. I don't get into it. My kids actually have it on their phones. The computer we do have here is dial-up, and it takes you forever to get online.

Do you have a favorite quote?

Actually, I do. It's the one that's on that cup. She's drinking from my cup.

(My photographer reads from the cup: "Accentuate the positive and eliminate the negative.")

Jiminy Cricket. That's my favorite cup. I drink out of that cup every morning.

How long have you had that cup?

Oh my gosh, forever. ■

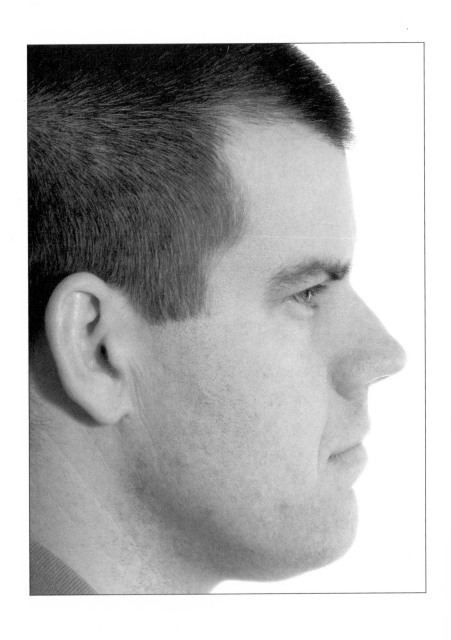

I struggle with sin every day

Marty Bascom

Born: January 2, 1973
Where: Springfield, VT
Siblings: One brother, older
College: Vermont Technical College
Degree: No (attends Southern Seminary theology courses in MA)
Married: Yes; three kids
Job: Pastor; also runs a lawn-care service

> Before I interview Marty Bascom, I email him and ask if he could put on a clerical collar for photographs. "I don't have a clerical collar," he says. Nor did he go to seminary school. A Southern Baptist, he sounds light-hearted, liberal, and funny. When I enter his small white church on Route 14 in East Randolph on a sunny March morning, the pews are buffed, the altar sparse, and Bascom, sticking his head out of an upstairs window, looks like a movie projectionist. He says hello, he'd be right down. We're soon seated on very small chairs in a Sunday School room, knees raised, and talking.

Could you describe for me what you do?

My daughter who goes to pre-school was asked by her teacher what I did, and she said I mowed lawns. Which is what I do. I'm not embarrassed or ashamed that I'm a pastor, but I don't introduce myself as Reverend Bascom. I feel that one of the strengths God's given me is I'm pretty much like everybody else.

Where did your religious training come from?

I grew up in the church . . . going to a church in Springfield. And when I moved to Kentucky, I was going to church there. When I interviewed for the church here, I met with some people. They were a pretty small group, and they weren't very fussy. After I moved here, I started attending seminary in Northboro, Massachusetts, a week-end seminary; I make trips, occasionally, down there to take classes.

It sounds like you came in through the back door of the church, so to speak. But you said you were raised in the Baptist Church.

I've been in the Baptist Church all my life. It's actually Southern Baptist. Now I'm learning a lot of different flavors of Baptist.

When did you take over the pulpit here?

It was eight years ago, this August. I had preached a time or two in Kentucky, but mostly I worked with the youth. My first sermon here was down the road, in a tent. They rented a tent to have a tent crusade. So that was different. We had some visitors; I think we had fifteen to seventeen people. Over the last couple months, on a Sunday morning, we have been averaging about a hundred people, including children. We also have Children's Church. When I get ready to preach, the children go upstairs.

One of the things that kind of spurred me on to come back to Vermont is while I was in Kentucky, I went to a conference with a pastor from Georgia. While we were there, in *USA Today*, I noticed an article titled "Unchurched America." At that time Vermont was the second most unchurched state in the nation. Now we're number one. It really intrigued me to think, I live in a community, roughly fifty-five thousand people, and there are about 130 churches. I thought, Maybe this isn't where I'm supposed to stay.

You thought you should come back to your roots?

Yeah.

So, how did the congregation grow? Do you take credit for that?

(Marty shifts in his small chair, scrunching and loosening his face as he thinks.) The first thing—and you probably expect a preacher to say this—I attribute it to God bringing people here. One of the verses in the Bible that has been really crucial for me for being in a spiritually-challenging place is Jesus said, "I will build my church." I've just believed He means the universal Church. He doesn't necessarily mean the East Randolph Baptist Church. And I have believed that that was a promise. And thought if I'm faithful, I'm just going to trust that things will work out.

They've been challenging at times. The first year here I was the age of the children and grandchildren of most of the parishioners. That was difficult for everybody. But one of the things that has really been neat here that I never saw in the churches I grew up in is the genuineness, and the authenticity, of people here. Pretty much what you see is what you get. I mean, sure, we don't know everything about everybody. But there just seem to be people coming together to learn about the Bible. Do life together! That's really the way the church started in Acts, chapter 2.

There's been a pretty neat thing, what I call "regular Vermont men just actually enjoying bringing their families to church." I never saw that as a kid; it was mainly the moms bringing the kids. But we got carpenters and electricians and, you know, excavators and builders. But we also have businessmen and the very educated. We got a fellow who's a lawyer, and [we've got] a meteorologist. I mean, it's just an amazing melting pot of people from different denominational backgrounds and educational levels. It's been a cool thing to see. I attribute it to trying to be simple in our approach. Not get all caught up in some of the stuff that people get caught up in. Just simply try to teach people the Bible, and live by it.

When I lived in Nashville for a while, Southern Baptist was pretty popular there.

Ahhh, that was the deal! (Marty turns happy as a boy, laughs loudly.) That was like the Mecca!

But no dancing. No singing. Are you that kind of Baptist Church?

No. Now, years ago there was this sweet lady in this church. And when she and her husband came to church, that was the deal: no bull, no cards, no dancing. That's not preached from the pulpit here.

Why don't you dance?

I'm not good at it. The last time I did it I was three sheets to the wind. (More laughter.)

Another time in my life!

During your years here, what was the high point, or time, when you felt closest to God?

When I almost got fired. I'd been here about a year . . . (and he trails off, goes silent until I ask him what happened). I think what happened is—I'm a big believer because the Bible teaches you this, teaches you that God will put you through trials to test ya. I think that's exactly what happened to me. I've always been in kind of a struggle with being a man pleaser, because I like people. I don't want to make them upset. But I realized that part of what God's calling is is to lead. The Greek word for pastor is shepherd. I don't know much about sheep, but I know that God's called me to shepherd his people in this congregation. And some people don't want to be led. At times that means you have to make some hard decisions. I made some hard decisions that I knew could possibly have some serious ramifications. But through that whole season is when the church really started to grow, and I think it was like God was saying to me, "Do you want to lead the church or not?"

You were in sort of a crucible.

Yeah. I personally don't believe God audibly speaks to people anymore.

In the Bible He did. But I believe God has given us the Bible as his revelation; he doesn't need to speak to us anymore. He's given us everything we need in that book. But I found myself in the parsonage, next door, literally in tears, asking if I should get out of Dodge. And in the closest thing I've ever hard to an audible voice . . . an impression on my heart . . . God said, "You stay, until I say go." And it was like—(he snaps his fingers.) From that moment on, everything changed . . . cause I knew this is where I'm supposed to be and I need to be faithful until I'm not here anymore.

What was your low point?

Low points. When I get focused on myself and miss the vision, the calling, the purpose of me being here. You know, pity party . . . woe is me . . . I didn't sign up for this. Basically, that kind of self-centered thinking. I can't point to a date and time, but it all relates to that: me thinking about myself.

We've had hard economic times lately. Do you think this is a dark time, a dark era shadowed by the economics we live with?

I don't. I don't even know if I should mention this, but I'm going to. This church has done financially very well the last couple years. We've been able to make a lot of improvements to the building. Purchase the property across the street and make some renovations. We've been able to help a lot of people in the community, both in the church and outside of the church. So, as I look from the church lens, it's quite the opposite, which I realize makes no sense. But that's what happened. Umm . . . are there people in our congregation struggling? Sure. People without jobs? Sure. Struggling a lot . . . yeah! But I guess, for me, being a man of faith and really leaning on what the Bible says, I think it's a great opportunity for people in the church to realize that our hopes should not be rooted in our 401(k)s. I realize that probably sounds like a spiritual thing to say, but I'm convinced of that. I think it's a great opportunity for us. And maybe it's going to bring back some of what we've lost, in that people will actually cross the road for a loaf of bread.

The other day I interviewed a parole officer in St. Albans. He said that bad times, a bad economy, create a lot of criminals. Have you found that people in your church have been getting in trouble?

No. From what I've observed in the last couple years things have gotten better. I realize that probably everything I say is the polar opposite of what's normal. Obviously, I don't know everything going on. But I've had the privilege to know most of the families very well. So no, I see less of that, not only in the congregation but in this community. Another thing I see, which goes back to the Vermonter spirit, is people in Vermont are so able to do so many different things. They get creative.

Like the local-food movement? (He looks perplexed, like, What is that?) You know, local food. Farms-to-food programs. Are they big around here?

In the church there are several gardeners. There's one lady in particular grows a very large garden. Sunday, after church, she'll whip up her trunk and hand out veggies and stuff. There's a lot of sharing. Not exactly what you're talking about, but I hear more people talking about having a garden together. My wife just had her gall bladder out and the doctor said, "One of the greatest things you could do is eat food grown as close to you as possible." He wasn't necessarily saying, "Organic." He was saying the less hands it goes through the better it is. For us, for health reasons, we're probably going to be looking into more of that.

What do you think's going to happen the next five years? Where would you like to see the state go?

I think we will be thinking about food differently; we got to have that. We're going to have to figure out creative ways to save money and help each other out. We probably won't be able to keep doing the things we have been doing. I don't look at that as a bad thing because all of us need to make adjustments in our lives, especially if we're concerned about our neighbors. I try not to say too much about politics and government, because I'm very opinionated. I know that even the folks I don't agree with work hard, and I wouldn't want to do their jobs. As you probably figured, I'm extremely conservative. By and large this state does a lot of things that would be a little different than what I would choose. I'm still thankful to live here, even though some of the decisions made in Montpelier wouldn't be decisions that I would make. But they're still people who, I think, are serving the state, and they're elected officials.

(He blows out his lips in a forced exhalation.) I'm a firm believer that the moral climate of our country is not to be set by the government. It's to be set by the church. Although I do agree with some of the decisions that are made in Washington and Montpelier, I don't think that's their job.

I don't know if this is a good story, but I had the opportunity, shortly after I moved here, to go share a devotional for the House of Representatives.

Vermont does that. It was just a few minute thing, and I prayed a lot about it—Oh, what in the world could I say . . . I don't know anything about politics . . . I'm a kid! But what I did was I took the opportunity to ask forgiveness on behalf of Christians, and myself, who had been very critical of the government. I noticed that nobody listened to me until I said that. Then they saw that I was trying to say that I don't think a lot of things that have been done in the name of Christianity have been what Jesus would do.

Yeah, I would love it if everyone in government had the same Christian convictions I do. But I know that's not reality. Would I vote for someone with the same convictions? Sure I would. I understand that's probably not going to happen. But then again it's not Montpelier's job to raise my children nor to help me pastor the church. I hope we're not ever taxed, but if we are, we are. I don't worry about it. I trust God for all those things. I know it's probably not reality not to have political parties, but it'd be nice. Because who cares? I will vote for you if I feel you're best for the state. Not because you're an elephant or a donkey.

Where would you like to see your own life go in the future?

I'm hoping I can spend all of my ministry in Vermont. And possibly at this church, at least until my children get out of high school. I really have a dream to see these rural, beautiful churches in Vermont once again have worship services on Sunday morning. If God gives me the opportunity, that's what I'll probably spend my later years doing. Trying to revitalize meeting houses that once had the word of God preached, people coming together praying, caring for their community. That's my dream for Vermont, to see that happen. I know the Great Awakenings came to New England once, and I'm hoping that someday that'll happen again.

I'm also concerned that the people who love Vermont aren't going to be able to stay here. The guy who's making ten bucks an hour, who grew up here. It's a bummer to think that a guy whose grandparents lived here might not be able to stay without living in a box somewhere. At the same time it's the government's job to figure that out, totally. I'm concerned for my children. I have a dream that two of my boys would someday want to do this gig. If they don't, that's fine. But if they wanted to stay here, it's a tough place to live. It's awesome to live here, but you got to be able to eat and heat and have a roof over your head. I haven't lived all over the country by any means. I've traveled some, but who wouldn't want to live here?

Your community, could you describe your community for me?

Well, my relationship with God comes first. But my family won't take a back seat to the church. I will be called lazy before I'll sacrifice my family. But the church hasn't made me make that choice. They've been very gracious and kind. I want my kids to love the church because they saw it's a profit to the family, not because it took their dad away every night of the week.

I think if we read scripture right, it'll help us lead our families right. Be the fathers, be the mothers, whatever. Christ likens his relationship to the church, in which he died on the cross, to a marriage. He tells me, in scripture, in Ephesians: "Husbands, love your wives, as Christ loved the church." If I have that kind of sacrificial attitude for my wife, my family's going to function pretty well, because it's going to be a sacrificial life. I'm not going to play golf—I don't play golf. I'm not going to go have fun with the boys. I'm going to stay home and help, get the kids ready for bed or whatever. The problem is that a lot of Christians aren't living like they're instructed to in the Bible. They're calling it Christian living. But it's not! It's humanistic Christian living. (He laughs forgivingly.)

What about the non-church people in town? Are you the kind of pastor who goes and knocks on the doors of people who haven't joined the church?

No. I try to be normal, whatever that means. I married a couple Saturday that have never set foot in the church, other than for their wedding and when we met. I told them, "If I perform your wedding, I want to be a part of your life. That doesn't mean I expect you in church on Sunday." I know everybody in this community doesn't come to church here. I'm not an idiot! Yet, I would like to think that if someone lives in this community and has a real issue or concern for a sick loved one, or the loss of a loved one, they would know we cared and would love to come alongside them.

I think in the last few years we've gotten a lot better reputation. I hear stuff; I don't know if any of it's true. But one of my first interactions at the post office when I came here was with a woman who doesn't live in the community anymore. She looked at me and said, "So, how long are you going to be here?" It was like, Wow! I mean, I'm like gun shy as it is, and this woman's my neighbor and asking me this question . . . and I'm like, "I hope a long time."

We've been talking mostly about positive stuff. What really irritates you? Makes you grind your teeth?

There is a way the Bible tells us to function as Christians. It bothers

me when we don't do that. It hurts the testimony of the church. That might be the most diplomatic way to say that. Fortunately, that hasn't been a big problem here. In the last few years I've seen the church function pretty well. Perfectly, no . . . we're never going to see that—too filled with humans! Yet when it's functioning the way that God laid it out for us in scripture, I've seen things happen . . . you know, reconciliation in people's lives . . . just amazing. What gets under my skin is when we get petty and miss out on the opportunity to meet the needs of other people through the truth of God's word. I don't get that upset about civil unions or gay marriage. I'm not going to march on Montpelier's lawn over that. The decision that our government has made is contrary to my convictions to what I understand the scriptures say. But I think the church gets in the wrong types of disputes at times.

One of the guys I interviewed, Nathan Chates, is gay. What would you say to him?

I was in California about a year ago at a pastor's conference, and in LA this is obviously a big issue. The conference was at a church that believes homosexuality is in conflict with the teaching of God's word, just like any other sexual sin. I had a conversation with a guy and I said, "I'm struggling with this. I'm struggling with how to deal with this." And he gave me some very good advice. "Now, when you go to a person who is homosexual, you go to them as one struggling sinner to another. You don't stand on a six-foot platform. You love them, yet you don't slide on your convictions."

Now, if a homosexual couple came to this church, I'd be glad they came. They wouldn't be able to join the church, but I'm not going to shoo them out the door to hear God's word. But the same would be true of a straight couple, a guy that's swamped in some other thing—maybe he's a compulsive liar and can't tell the truth. I mean, I don't see God's word divides between this struggle with this sin. I think the teaching of scripture is very clear on that. All sin separates from God. That's why Jesus died on the cross, to reconcile us back to God. So, if I start categorizing sins because I don't like these type of people—I don't like liars—that's my conviction. It really has nothing to do with God.

I struggle with sin every day. I believe that I have been forgiven by the grace of God, because of the cross of Jesus Christ. One of my heroes of the faith is the apostle Paul, possibly the greatest Christian who ever walked the face of the earth. Under the inspiration of God he wrote half the New Testament . . . more than half. He's the giant in the faith. And he said, in Romans 7, "I do things that I hate. I know they're wrong, and there's this war raging within my flesh, to struggle." Yet in the next chapter in the Bible he spelled out his identity in Christ. He said, "Even though I'm struggling with this" . . . and he wasn't specific on what it was, the sin he was struggling with—it could have been lust, could have been anger. We don't know what it was, and it's irrelevant, because we all have the struggle. But he said he recognized, and this is one of my favorite verses in the Bible, Romans 8:1: "There is therefore now no condemnation for those who are in Jesus Christ." That's been very helpful to me because I clearly understand my struggle with all types of sin. I struggle with anger, I struggle with how I want to smack church people over the head, I struggle with all those things. I believe that I'm forgiven by the grace of God and placed in the loving care of God. The Bible talks about the Christian being adopted into God's family. I believe I'm secure in Him, yet there's a struggle. I'm very open about my struggle from the pulpit. If there's anything that maybe God has given me that's really helped me, it's that He's given me a clear understanding that I'm no better than any person in that congregation who walks through those doors. God's been gracious and kind to me, and I want to share that from the pulpit. I don't stand up on the pulpit and say, "Oh I didn't sin this week! So now I've got something to say!" Man, I probably struggled with sin five times that morning.

If you're a physical man, an intellectual man, and an emotional man, which of you is the top driver?

It's not intellectual—that's not me! One of my good friends in Kentucky—this is very embarrassing, but it's funny. One of my good friends in Kentucky I played softball with, he said, "You're just like a woman." So, as much as I hate to say it, I would probably say emotional. I'd like to say physical . . . and I could . . . but I don't know if it would be true.

I'd like to ask you my classic Vermont questions: Have you ever milked a cow?

Yeah. The last cow I remember milking—I didn't milk the whole cow, just played around with it—was in Springfield, Vermont, at Bull Run Farm at my wedding reception. This was the fun wedding. The serious one was in Kentucky. But when we came back to Vermont a couple of months later, that was the fun one.

How about tapping trees, making maple syrup?

Last year I helped a guy at church do that. I tapped the trees, and we collected sap too.

You put away food, so any canning?

Not so much. I'm going to make a note to myself: I need to can. My mom did that.

How about hunting, fishing?

I'm one of those guys who takes the gun for a walk. I've never killed a deer. I've shot a woodchuck. I think I shot a beaver once. It was illegal, so maybe I shouldn't have done it. Actually, maybe the statute of limitations is passed by now. You know, I did get to spend some time in a courtroom in Montpelier after illegally discharging a firearm. A friend of mine at VTC [Vermont Technical College], when I went there, got a new rifle. He said, "Let's go up on the back hill and shoot my new rifle." He was a real Vermonter. Needless to say, somebody reported us, and we got ourselves in a bit of a predicament. That's my big outlaw story.

How about winter sports?

I've gone skiing once this year. I went to Pico. Never been; it was great.

I went for a hard half day. It was one of the best days skiing I ever had. I've gone ice skating twice.

Are you a Vermont history buff?

I'd like to say I am. I love Vermont. It's where I was born but I'm not a history buff. I would like to sit on a porch, with a root beer, with a good old Vermonter, and listen to him share what it was like.

Cultural stuff. Are you a music or movie fan? You read a lot of books?

This is where I get really boring. My wife's a reader. I try to read books that will help me be a better father, better husband, better pastor. Movies? I'm too practical. I don't want to drop thirty bucks to go to the movies and pay child care. It bugs my wife; she likes to go to the movies.

Do you use Facebook yet? Does your church use social media?

I have to confess, I am on Facebook. My goal is not to do text messaging. I receive them, but I have yet to send one. For me, that's like getting to the brink of really getting obnoxious. But probably in a year, when our cell phone contract's renewed, I'll be sucked into that too.

Do you have a favorite quote?

Psalms 130, verse 3 and 4. That really is a driving verse for me. I also have a bunch of index cards on humility. I have them nailed to my bookshelf, and I try to look at them pretty regularly because if there's anything's that going to kill a person, it's pride. I realize that to even say that runs the risk of looking prideful. (He laughs at himself again.) It is important.

Do you believe in evolution?

I definitely do not believe in evolution. In the beginning of the Bible is the Book of Genesis, and the beginning verse says, "God created . . . ." I believe that if a person doesn't hold to that, the whole rest of the Bible is corrupt. There's no sense in even reading it; it's *just* a book. My conviction is that if I don't believe God created out of nothing, which is spelled out in the first chapter of the Bible, to me the whole rest of the Bible is corrupt. I'm pretty dogmatic about scripture. I will waver on a lot of things, but that's not one of them. I'm not a Darwin hater or anything like that. I just believe, you know, the Bible clearly says, God created out of nothing, and that's what I hold to.

If you go to the zoo and look at chimpanzees, you don't think they're related to us?

No. There's chimpanzees and there's us. I'm not going to go up on a hill and make a case against evolution. I appreciate what you believe. I don't believe the same thing. I think that gets dangerous, when we start thinking, I'll take a little of this, and a little of this, and mix them together, and maybe we can make everybody happy. It doesn't work!

Can you summarize your life over the last eight or nine years?

When my wife and I moved here, we had no children. Now we have three. I had never pastored a church before; now I have for almost eight years. For the first time in my life I can honestly say—I hate to say I found my calling because that just sounds so weird. But I've found something I enjoy doing, and I actually get paid to do it. I mean, I love what I do. There are days it's rough, but overall I just smile at the fact I get to do something that I had no idea I'd ever be able to do. I meet so many people who just struggle going to work . . . "Ah, I just don't want to go back to that place" . . . and I feel so grateful.

You like getting up in the morning.

Oh yeah! ∎

You make sure they follow the rules

Chris Billado

Born: September 2, 1983
Where: St. Albans, VT
Siblings: Three brothers; one older, two younger
College: University of Vermont
Degree: Sociology and Political Science
Married: Yes
Job: Community corrections officer

Chris Billado lives in one of those Vermont towns you seldom pass through unless you have business there. A farming community experiencing the same hard times as many other Vermont farming communities, Franklin has its share of busted, decaying barns, sentinels of the not-so-distant past, and washboard roads, several of which lead to the Canadian border. I find Chris living temporarily in a new house on a dirt road. From the porch he can see his own new house, which is nearing completion on land given to him and his wife by her grandmother. A rather stern but straightforward guy, Chris was raised nearby in Swanton and now is in his third year as a community corrections officer for the Vermont Department of Corrections. We sit at the kitchen counter with a view of meadows sprawling to the north beneath gray, somber clouds.

We're in this relatively bad economy. How has this tough economy affected you?

It really hasn't. We've been fortunate. My wife is in a very stable job—she's an RN, so she doesn't have to worry about losing her job. The same with me; as the economy turns bad, there's more criminals. There's more criminal activity, so therefore it's job security for myself.

Then the economy has been positive for you?

Yes and no. It hasn't affected me in my job but it could. There's always the potential that my job could get cut. I could be on the unemployment line. Hopefully, we're on a rebound and it's not going to happen. But I don't think we are; I think we're behind the ball. That always seems to be the mode in Vermont; we're always two steps behind everybody else. Unemployment is at an all-time high. That's a key indicator of a recession right there.

Let's talk about your job and its opportunities.

My official title is community corrections officer. I work for the

Vermont Department of Corrections, the St. Albans probation and parole office. There's three of us that do the job I do. Then you've got the probation officers. There's anywhere between fifteen to eighteen probation officers. Then you've got supervisors and a district manager. In our office we have between twenty and twenty-five individuals. I've worked there for three years. Before that I worked out of the Northwest State Correctional Facility. I was a correctional officer. In the jail, I was basically keeping inmates in line. You know, there's rules on the outside and there's rules on the inside. You just make sure they're following the rules on the inside and take the appropriate action to correct them if they're not.

And what do you do now?

A community corrections officer is, basically, a field probation officer. People get released from jail after a minimum sentence; they're on conditional re-entry and they have conditions they have to follow. As a community corrections officers I enforce those conditions and make sure they're being followed appropriately. That entails, you know, going house to house to house in these people's private setting—sometimes it's a little intrusive, but that's my job.

So, if I'm on parole and I'm back in the public realm, do I meet with you?

You have to meet with your probation or parole officer at the office in an office setting. Me, I'll see you seven days a week if I chose. Twenty-four hours a days, seven days a week. That's part of the condition, that you have to be readily accessible. The whole point of probation is to reintegrate you into society to become a successful member. If that wasn't the case, you'd see the prison population skyrocketing, and you'd have a lot more crime. You'd have individuals who would be released from jail with absolutely no reintegration into society and [they would often go] right back to square one. I have a high-risk case load, anywhere from a DLS (Driving While License Suspended) all the way up to Murder 1. It's anything and everything.

How many people are you seeing at any one time?

That gets into specifics that I'm not a hundred percent sure I can talk about. That's walking a fine line between what I can talk about and what I can't talk about.

Okay. But you're busy?

Yeah, we're busy. We're *very* busy.

When you have a new person added to your case load, do you have a gut feel about how they're going to work out?

I try not to do that. I just take it as it is. Everything is based on how they act in a community. In a very short period of time you can tell. Are they going to actually try to change themselves or not? I usually do not go off on a gut feel, but sometimes we get returnees; they're back and we'll see how long they're going to be out this time.

Do you like this work?

Absolutely. I'm a people person. You know, I can talk to anybody in any situation. Before I started this career path, I worked in retail. That helps out a lot when I'm talking to people. Everyday is a different day. Unfortunately, sometimes it's more bad than good.

Is it true that the number of people going to prison increases during a bad economy?

You actually see more people being placed on probation because in a bad economy you're not talking violent crimes. You're talking property crimes. You're talking low-risk stuff, drug activity, so-called victimless crimes. People end up getting a probation sentence. The judges have to be—I don't know how to say it—they have to play with the system. If everyone that's got a drug conviction is thrown into jail, you're taking up the bed space of violent people that should be in jail versus someone who shouldn't be there. The judges are trying to put non-violent people on probation. Yeah, they need a little supervision, but they don't need to go to jail. So we try to fix it through probation first. If your probation gets violated, then ultimately you end up in jail. Dealing with violations of probation, it's ultimately the judge's decision.

When you're growing up, did you ever get in trouble with cops?

I can't say I didn't do stuff that I could have gotten in trouble, but I was fortunate enough so I didn't get too out of hand.

It seems that fate comes into play. Some sixteen or seventeen year olds get busted at a keg party in the woods or get a DUI, and they just get on the wrong path.

A lot of people I went to high school with are exactly what you're talking about. They're still not in trouble with the law, it's just that they chose the wrong path. In some situations they have family support and they have the means to lead a successful life, and they just chose not to. My class at Missisquoi Valley Union—and my wife can attest to it too—should have been, on paper, a successful class. They're not. I mean, there are quite a few people in my class that are doing very well for themselves, but the jocks went off and played sports and did their thing, you know, went into sports medicine and stuff like that. Their freshman year in college, that first taste of freedom killed them, they're still at home living with their moms and dads.

Are your parents from Vermont?

My dad was born in Richford. He was raised in Richford, moved to Enosburg and then came to Swanton. My mom's been in Swanton all her life. My dad works at IBM in the manufacturing end of things. He's dodged every job cut there, so he's pretty fortunate. My two younger brothers work there now. My mom works at Missisquoi Valley Union as a nurse's aid.

Are you a Vermont history buff?

If you asked me that five years ago, probably I could spew off a lot of Vermont history, just because I was in college. But the work that I do now, it's more concentrated on law and how to interact with people. So am I interested in Vermont history a little bit? Can I spew off a bunch of Vermont history to you? Probably not.

Let's talk a little about Vermont politics. Are you much of a political person?

Since I've worked for the state, I'm directly affected by politics. Two or three times a year you hear about state cuts. Am I going to get on the list or am I not going to get on the list? That's directly affected by the people in the legislature saying, "This is where we need to trim the fat." I don't think cuts should be occurring in corrections; we're already stretched pretty thin. To cut more jobs in corrections could be dangerous. As far as where the cuts should go, a lot of people say welfare. For me to say they should cut there would be unfair, just because I don't know how welfare works.

Who makes up your community? Who do you trust?

My wife and I joke that our only friends are our family. And it's true. When we have days off, we're spending time with our families. We have a few friends that we hang out with every now and then, but our support group is our family.

Do you miss your old buddies?

Not one bit . . . not one bit. I would feel more comfortable calling up a friend from college and going and hanging out at their house than I would hanging out with a friend from high school.

Do you go to church?

Three brothers

Not as much as I should. My wife does, my wife goes every Sunday. I'm a Catholic, she's a Catholic. But she goes to the Methodist Church. I go to the Methodist and the Catholic churches. I'm not a strong practicing Catholic. I figure, you go to church, you go to church.

Are there job opportunities around here for people in their twenties?

In Franklin County, no. You want to work in the private sector, head south. Go to Burlington or get out of the state. Private sector jobs in Vermont are far and between. If I was to lose my job and get on the unemployment line, I don't know what I'd do. My wife is always telling me to go back to school and be a nurse. I don't know if I would do that, but I'd probably go to school to do something else. There's jobs, you always have your factory jobs. Right in St. Albans you've got a few factories. You've got Peerless clothing, you've got the chocolate factory, and Ben & Jerry's. Those are nine or ten dollar an hour jobs, and they don't direct hire any more. You've got to go through a temp agency to be hired. So you're actually being employed by a temp agency and you get no benefits. If you're going to maintain a house on your own and pay your taxes, the cost of living is just way too high for that type of work.

Have many of your former buddies in Swanton found good jobs?

Some have. But my closest friends in high school are just not doing well for themselves at all. It has to do with the choices they made when they graduated from high school. A lot of them got into drugs real fast and they stayed with it. They're still with it and they can't afford to do anything on their own.

In this last decade what was your low point?

I graduated from college, I wasn't utilizing my degree. I was thinking, I just spent forty thousand dollars on my education and I'm working in a retail store. I was working at Best Buy.

So tell me how you went from Best Buy to the correctional facility?

My parents kind of kicked me in the ass. My dad usually won't kick you hard, my mom will. She's the one to get you going. I remember, it was 2005 and I said, "I'm going to work at Best Buy for the next year, and if in a year I'm still working for Best Buy, I'm going to join the military." The next year came around and my mom said, "You're still working at Best Buy, why don't you join the military?" I said, "No, I'm still going to work at Best Buy." Then there was a management change at Best Buy. I didn't like it. It was time to do something.

I saw the correctional facility job posted online. I had reservations about working in a correctional facility because being a correctional officer isn't the most ideal job. But it was a foot in the door to somewhere. I applied and I went for the interview and they hired me on the spot. Within five months the community correction officer job came open and I applied for it and I got it. That's when I really decided, Yeah, probation and parole work is where I want to be.

What was your high point the past decade?

Right now, building my house. I didn't really think I'd be able to build a house. My wife's grandmother gave us the land so that cut down a huge cost. We applied for a mortgage at eleven o'clock in the morning, and we were approved by four o'clock in the afternoon. We had a trailer, you know. It was cheap but nobody finances trailers. (Chris smiles for the first time.) We sold our trailer.

Ohhh, man, we put a lot of time in on our new house. All the ground work we did. We put in the septic ourselves, we put in the foundation ourselves. Everything basically from the ground down, we did ourselves. Then a contractor did the rest.

If there was one thing you could change in your life, what would it be?

I wouldn't change anything. I'm building a house right now, I'm married, I'm financially secure, I have a close-knit family, both my parents are alive, my wife's parents are alive. You know, I'm pretty fortunate.

You like living in Vermont?

Umm . . . I'm not a hundred percent sure on that. In the winter time you hear me swearing and saying, "I wish I lived somewhere warmer." For twenty-six years of my life I lived on a one-eighth acre lot, and if it wasn't for my family during that time, I'd probably have left the state. Actually, I had a job opportunity the first year I graduated from college to move to San Diego for Border Patrol. I ended up getting engaged to my wife, so I stayed. Now, being out here, I just look around and ask, Why wouldn't you stay? You've got all this land and it's peaceful out here, and there's no reason to leave. If I did leave, it would be because of the cold.

What pisses you off, what makes you mad?

Not a lot. Not a lot. I mean, you can't get pissed at work because you're dealing with a situation where failure happens more than success. I took the job and I knew what I was getting into. You can't get pissed off at that.

(He pauses, almost smiles.) If I let the little things bother me, I'd probably have a heart attack.

My standard Vermonter questions: You ever milk a cow?

I haven't.

How about making maple syrup?

On my wife's grandmother's farm; they have a sugar woods out there. Actually, for our wedding, we gave away maple syrup that we boiled ourselves.

How about canning food?

We make our own jam. We do pickles. But that's about it.

Hunting? Fishing?

(He gestures out the window towards the meadow.) If you stay long enough, you'll see about forty deer back here. I started when I was nine, and I've hunted ever since. I went a number of years without shooting a deer; it was very discouraging. The first deer I saw shot, it could have been my deer. I was young, I was probably ten years old, and my dad was sitting next to me. I had a little .410 shotgun on my lap. My dad is sleeping and I see a deer jump in front of me. I wake my dad and say, "Dad, there's a deer right there." It's an eight-pointer, and it's too far away for me to shoot with my .410, so my dad shoots him. I never shot my first deer until I started hunting out here in 2005.

We fish on Lake Champlain near the Tyler Place, where my dad has a boat. I did a lot of fishing last year in the boat. (Chris breaks a full smile.) Every story is a fish story, especially ones that you lose, because the biggest fish that you ever caught got away, right? My biggest was a thirty-one or thirty-two inch Northern, about fourteen pounds. We dropped anchor in about eight feet of water. I had on a Rattletrap lure.

What about the future? What are your concerns?

Jobs stability, obviously. That's always been the number one concern, especially now, having a mortgage, a good size mortgage. How far are the job cuts going to go? That's about it.

A few cultural questions. Are you a movie guy? Do you like to read?

I am a movie and video game guy. Ever since I picked up my first Atari, I haven't put it down. I still game an hour here and there. Not the way I used to. Back when I was younger, you could catch me for four or five hours on a rainy day in front of a TV. Now I don't have time. Yesterday, I played for maybe an hour because it was raining out.

Lately, I started reading some true crime stuff. I've just finished a book called *Under and Alone,* which is about an ATF [Bureau of Alcohol, Tobacco and Firearms] guy who went to a mongrel biker gang and got a bunch of arrests. It was a pretty good book. I'm actually reading *Angels and Demons* right now, the prequel to *The Da Vinci Code.* And I love music. Anything and everything but country. I'm not huge on rap either. I used to be back in my hoodlum days, I guess. (He chuckles.)

How about social media? Facebook?

I have a Facebook account. The only thing I use it for is a game called Farmville. I play Farmville daily. My wife laughs at me because we're in competition to see who can have a bigger and better farm. She plays, my mom plays, I've got a bunch of people from work who play Farmville.

Do you have a favorite quote?

Wow . . . I probably do. If I'm going to throw out a quote, I'm going to throw out a good one. I'd have to think about that.

(Later, Chris sends me a quote.)

You can't change the wind,
But you can adjust your sails.
—Anon ■

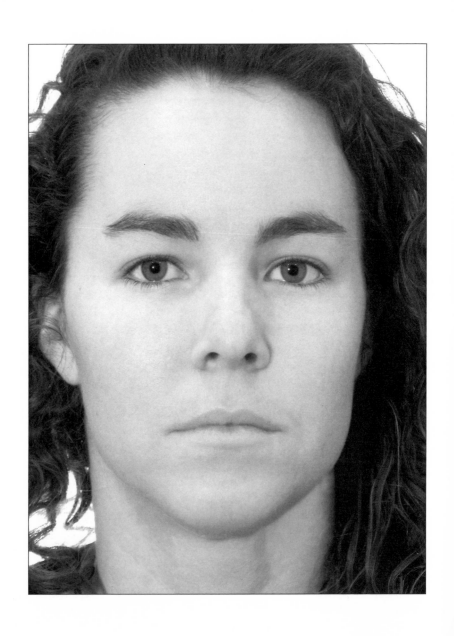

I majored in soccer

Eliza Bradley

Born: September 15, 1988
Where: Burlington, VT
College: University of Vermont
Degree: Communication Sciences
Siblings: One sister, older
Married: No
Job: Athlete; has future job as commodities trader

Eliza Bradley was a star soccer goalie in high school and went on to play division one soccer at the University of Vermont. "I majored in soccer," she says. "I played almost every single game from freshman to senior year." Twenty-one, full of optimism and high spirits, she is about to head off to London for a short stint at a cooking school and some travel. In the fall she starts a job as a grain trader for Ackerman Beardsley Bennett Inc. In her apartment in Burlington we sit down and talk about her years as an athlete, her quirky route to becoming a commodities trader, and her reasons for loving to cook

First, can you tell me why you love to cook?

I used to make tacos and sloppy joes for my parents and family. Then I really found more passion for cooking during the winter break of my freshman year in college. I was getting *Eating Well* magazine and I'd pick out a full menu and do appetizer, dinner, and dessert. That was when I kind of realized how much I enjoyed it. Being in the dorms, I realized how bad food can taste. Now I absolutely love cooking. I cook for my friends, and we have an awesome time enjoying the food.

And you're taking a cooking course in London?

I'm enrolled in a basic, four-week course in London. You learn knife skills. You learn interesting dishes. Mini-chocolate mousse cakes—I'm really excited about that. You do hands-on stuff, you learn about nutrition, planning a menu. I think, in the end, what we do is we cater an event for like fifty people.

My sister's been in London since November; she's learning the ropes. We're complete opposites, basically. She says she's so excited to get me there because I love, like, organization. Learning the tube schedules and how everything works. She's pretty sure she's done nothing right and there's a much faster way to get everywhere. We'll figure it out when I get there.

When you return, what's this opportunity you have waiting for you?

It's a grain-trading firm. We buy and sell commodities. Our job is to connect the big feed users to the small community farms and other big farms. We don't actually take any of the grain into our possession. If a truck load of grain shows up at our office, it would be a huge mistake.

How'd you jump from being an athlete and communications major to grain trader?

I really had no idea what I wanted to do in college; I was completely undeclared. But UVM has an interesting program; it's called TAP, an acronym for Teacher Advisor Program. Students with undecided majors in arts and sciences get an opportunity during the first semester to take these very small, really interesting classes. So I signed up. There were eleven kids in my class, which for a freshman is unheard of. The class was the Structure of Romance Languages. It was a very cool class. We basically looked at how the Romance languages were born and their interconnectivity. I was absolutely fascinated with this class and absolutely loved my teacher. And so I was looking at my schedule for the next semester and I asked, "Well, what else are you teaching?" She was teaching phonetics, so I was like, "All right, I'll dive into it!" So that was kind of how I whetted my appetite for communication sciences.

The grain-trading company was actually owned by one of my dad's best friends. When I was a freshman, and my dad realized I had time on my hands, he said, "Eliza, I'm going to get you a job." I started there just paying railroad invoices. Now I'm in charge of invoicing, and I can pretty much do every single job in the office.

For a lot of people the economic times have been dark. But it sounds like they've worked pretty well for you.

I've been extremely lucky, for sure. They always say, "It's not what you know, it's who you know." That's certainly worked out well for me. But, you know, I could have hated the job. It could have been torture for me the last four years. But I enjoy the whole business. The more I learn about it, the more I've become interested in it. I have a very good working relationship with the boss.

Working there, will grain trading take advantage of your skill set from college?

Yeah. I mean, being a student athlete in division one gives you a whole new perspective. It's utterly time consuming. A lot of times, like when you're absolutely exhausted from running sprints and stuff like that, you find yourself asking, "Why am I doing this?" A lot of people don't make it four years. It really instills a work ethic that is hard to match. Athletes have to be good time-management people because they're on the road. You have to be well-organized. And, you know, I got to be captain when I was a senior.

Once you get into the trading part of my job, you're dealing with numbers. It's controlled gambling to some extent. You have to know enough about the business and enough about where your grain is coming from to know that, Oh, Nebraska had horrible weather, so the crop's going to go down . . . in three months when they're harvesting, there's going to be less . . . so I want to buy it now, cheaper.

If you're a good grain trader, would you be a good carbon trader?

Yeah. Trading commodities, the good thing about it is that once you learn how to predict the future, the patterns and stuff, you can take it and you can go from trading grain to trading oil futures to carbon to any sort of commodity that you can come up with. I could go to New York, or I could go anywhere else, if I wanted to go anywhere else.

At UVM what percentage of your time was taken up by athletics?

Aah . . . I mean (blows out through her lips). It's hard to say because you could define it as just the time I spent on the practice field or you can define it as the time that I spent getting ready for practice. You throw in mental time and it's 99.9 percent. (She laughs.) I've certainly spent way more time playing and thinking about soccer than thinking about school. It's not because I was slacking off at school or anything like that, but just because athletics is an all-consuming adventure.

As a soccer goalie did you ever get hurt?

I, thankfully, only had one semi-major injury. I broke my hand. I only missed one-and-a-half games. I was okay with that.

How successful were your teams?

We were not very successful in terms of our overall record. A lot of times we had problems scoring. Scoring was our issue. So, yeah, that was probably it . . . if you don't score, you can't win. [But] I'm one of the goalies who has way more fun when I'm making thirty saves in a game than when

I make one, even if I get a shut out. I enjoyed playing when I was getting absolutely shelled.

My best year was probably my freshman year. I was on the all-conference freshman team. I won the defense Most Valuable Player award a couple times for the tournament that we host at UVM. I have the UVM record for most minutes played in a career, and I'm in the top five in every statistical goal-keeping category. So I had a pretty successful individual career, partly because in a lot of games we played in I was making a lot of saves.

Now that you're graduating, who makes up your community?

I've stayed good friends with the people I met on the soccer team, but from that I've expanded. I hang out with some of the rugby players and with other athletes. The athletic community within UVM is very tightly knit. For the most part athletes hang out with athletes . . . just because the time demands and those kinds of things make it hard for people to really understand what your schedule is really like, physically, mentally, and time-wise.

Do you consider yourself more a physical, intellectual or emotional person?

Umm . . . that's hard. I like to think I have a pretty good balance of all of them. I mean, obviously, sports are physical. Intellectually, I do crosswords and that kind of thing. And yeah, emotionally, hopefully, I'm not completely stunted. Sadly, I don't have a boyfriend right now.

Are you a Vermont history buff?

I can't say I'm a history buff. I'm kind of known by my friends for having a vast knowledge of random facts. Jeopardy, I'm going to get on Jeopardy when I'm older. In high school we usually dabbled in history in terms of what role Vermont played in the larger aspect of the United States or the world. I don't think I ever had a specific Vermont history class.

Are you interested in politics?

To some extent. When I got to UVM, I found it hard to be involved in what was going on because I was consumed with athletics. But I definitely have a general idea of what's going on, and I'd like to say I'm somewhat informed . . . but you never know. You can always be more informed on politics.

I learned in my political science class that states are always kind of a training ground for national ideas. So you have states like Vermont that legalize gay marriage and [try to] legalize marijuana. I think Vermont is usually more willing to go out on a limb than some other states. We always seem like we're kind of in on the discussion, on the forefront of everything. (She smiles and speaks in a low, self-reflective tone.) I don't really know how we got there.

The last ten years sound like they've been good for you. What about low points? Did you ever cry your heart out or wonder what you're doing with your life?

(Eliza thinks for a minute.) Oh, that's a tough question. Throughout high school I had two very different lives that I ran. I had my athletic career which was unbelievably successful. I played, you know, all the time. But I didn't always get along with all the popular people in my high school. I'll say the first two years in high school I could have erased from this decade. One of my best friends—I didn't meet her until I was a junior— once I met her, I was fine. So does that answer your question? (Following my answer no, she thinks, brow furrowed.) I don't know . . . I don't really know if I had a truly low—okay! I can . . . yeah . . . I got you. I can revise. I can revise my statement. So, when I was in seventh grade, one of my best friend's dad died suddenly. He was a very important influence on my life. So losing him was huge. But also, my friend, the way she reacted to it basically resulted in the end of my friendship. She had been my best friend since I was four. Then, all of a sudden, it was so shocking for her and so hard that I was just a constant reminder of him and what she had before. And I think what happened was she decided at that point she was going to cut that part of her life off and create a new version of her life. That is something that still affects me today and was a very, very trying time.

How old were you before you could put this into perspective?

I'd say probably around tenth grade. My family was very good friends with her family. But she became very closed off. Her mom became very closed. We drove to tournaments together, and I was still around her and still interacting with her and it was the same amount of time spent together in the relationship, but it was very different. Whenever someone dies you have to ask, "Okay, do I talk about this person any more?" And her response was not to talk about it at all. Every time that you brought something up, it became a giant elephant in the room. At that point, seventh and eighth grade, it's hard to know how to deal with that. She went to prep school, and our relationship ended. Because of the distance it was severed.

In retrospect, do you find this was a positive experience for you in any way?

Umm . . . (she sucks air through her teeth, wincing.) I think it taught me that as much as someone often wants to shut out that part and not talk about it, it's important for them to talk about it. I allowed my friend not to talk about that. I didn't confront her. I think that definitely shaped how she dealt with it, because I probably was one of the few people she could have talked to about it. I learned something. If that's a positive, yes, then I had some positive from it. But it's not an experience that I look back on and ever think anything good about.

What was a high point of the last decade?

Oh, high point—yeah! I won a few state championships . . . . I won soccer and lacrosse, both freshman and junior years. The experience of having that with all your teammates, knowing that you played a big role in creating that momentous occasion for your school and your community, was really cool.

Also, my mom is graduating from college this year; I'd say that is pretty cool. And going to see my sister graduate. After that, we drove across the country together, just my sister and I. My sister is my best friend. Driving across the country is really amazing. People are always saying, "I wanna go to Europe, I wanna go there." But there are *really* cool places in the U.S.

I'm going to ask you my standard Vermont questions: Have you ever milked a cow?

One of my cousins has a dairy farm, so I've done the whole dairy farming thing. I got to ride in the tractor a few times. We had to, like, clean the stalls out. I didn't mind it. I've become immune to the smell of manure, which is something I feel like a true Vermonter has to be.

Ever make maple syrup?

I've boiled it, I've tapped the trees, I've fixed the lines, I've done it all. I actually make maple pecan pie.

How about putting food by, canning?

Yup. My mom does a lot of that. Dilly beans were my favorite, growing up. They're green beans in vinegar with dill and stuff like that. You crack open one of those and they're so good.

What about hunting, fishing?

I've done a lot of fishing. We have a house in Maine, so I fished a bunch in Maine. I'm trying to learn how to fly-fish. I've shot a rifle, but I've never shot a rifle at an animal. And I've shot a bow and arrow but never at an animal either.

Winter sports. Do you snowboard?

I snowboard, I ski, I snowshoe.

What do you think of Burton moving its manufacturing to China? (I'm referring to the iconic Vermont snowboard company.) Are you aware of this?

Noooo . . . *what?*

It was just announced this week.

I'm shocked by that. Wow . . . I don't know what to think about that. I love Burton. That's a bummer.

In the future what would you like to see happen in Vermont?

I think my only concern is the huge development. You know, fields that were vast. Taft Corners in Williston was an entire field when I was ten, and now I'm twenty and it's huge box stores. I feel we need to keep it rural. Living in Charlotte, we all had at least ten acres of land. I enjoy Burlington as a city and I've really enjoyed living here, but I think that my biggest fear would be that we allow suburbia to expand way past where it needs to be.

The health of Lake Champlain is also a concern. Zebra muscles and algae infestations and that kind of thing. The more zebra muscles there are, the clearer the lake is because they actually eat all the algae. But then you have to worry about their razor sharp edges tearing your feet to bits. Growing up near the lake and enjoying the pristine environment is something that I would like my kids to enjoy.

Do you like to read, watch TV?

I like both. I try to read before I go to bed every night. I read action novels, I'm a big *Harry Potter* fan, I love *Harry Potter*. That's kind of a cultural phenomenon that grew up as I grew up. I really liked the book *Freakonomics*. I like books that make you think of the world around you. Also Malcolm Gladwell's *Blink*, and [Jonah Lehrer's] *How We Decide*. They kind of interact with what I've studied in communication sciences. They make you think about things that you do every day that you kind of take for granted, and they put them in a new light. If I'm not going to just immerse myself and shut off my brain and read an action novel, I definitely like those kinds of thinking books.

With music I like everything. I used to not like country, but I live with two people who came from the West. One from Idaho, one from Colorado. So I've listened to a lot of country and it actually has some merit to it. I really don't like punk music, the hardcore screaming stuff. I'm not a big fan of that.

How about social media? Are you a social media fan?

I deleted my Facebook account a couple years ago because I was tired of it. I definitely look at the computer a lot and go to YouTube and I love Pandora, but I guess that's not really social media. I wouldn't say I'm one of those people that is absolutely obsessed by this. I don't have a Twitter account.

(From an adjacent room a roommate listening to us pipes up: "You're on your iPhone all the time!")

(Eliza laughs, blushes.) I love my iPhone. I have apps galore. I use the Internet, I use texting. I always say that the three companies from which I would buy pretty much everything they would make are Apple, Burton, and Nike. Now I have to wonder about Burton. Nike, I had to get back on their bandwagon. But Burton. (She moans.) I can't believe that.

Do you have a favorite quote?

I have a lot of movies that I can quote from. You've got the bunny scene in *Monty Python and the Holy Grail.* (Adopts a high, squeaky voice.) "It's joos a little 'abbit." (Then changes her tone.) "Wroight! One 'abbit stew comin' up!" (A third voice change.) "Did you see 'at? 'E bit its 'ead wroight off." That's some of my favorite stuff. Funny quotes, they're my favorite. I don't have a momentous, life-shaking quote that really guides my life. ∎

I wasn't out until I went to college

Nathan Chates

Born: April 1, 1985
Where: St. Albans, VT
Siblings: Two, older brother and younger brother
College: Marlboro College
Degree: Biology
Married: No; has a partner
Job: In-store computer technician

Nathan Chates lives in a third-floor walk up in a brick building over-looking Taylor Park in downtown St. Albans. A big, soft guy in black with a chain hanging from his belt, he wears glasses ("I'm mostly blind without my glasses"), owns a pet snake ("He's a Colombian red-tail boa"), and has a habit of intertwining his fingers and rubbing his thumbs together as he talks. Though it's a cool day in February, he's barefoot. We sit in large, lounge-like chairs facing computer monitors, probably from Staples, where he works.

Could you describe your job for me?

I'm the in-store technician who does the actual work on computers, be it repairs, software installs, whatever. I also interact with customers, talk with them, help them find the computer solutions. I do everything from that to stocking shelves.

Where'd you pick up your technical know-how?

Umm . . . .my family didn't have enough money to have a computer back when. My parents were divorced, my mother was single and trying to raise three kids, doing college herself, and all that. We lived in Highgate. That's where I grew up: East Highgate. I can't remember if my father got his computer first, or my uncle—I think it was my father because it was Windows 3.1. I toyed around. I just spent hours going through the computer, just trying to look and see how stuff worked, figuring things out. Just the way my mind works and the way my personality is, it's not difficult for me to figure things out. So I just kind of picked it up here and there and I did some stuff on my own and I was very problem-solver oriented.

A number of your peers say we're in a difficult economic time. Do you think we're drifting downward economically?

I haven't seen too much hard times. I mean I kind of have, I kind of haven't. The tricky part was when I started working at Staples, before all this happened; I never really had a good idea of how things worked in retail. The whole time I've been at Staples, all I've seen in our store is increases, so I haven't felt the negative effect of the economy much. On top of that I grew up with, like, little or no money. All the time we were on welfare when I was younger. So anything compared to that is an improvement to me. Therefore, in my own little world here, I think, even if I only have five dollars to spend, all my bills are paid, I have food, I have electricity, I have things people don't have like cable, and I surf the Internet. (He glances at the array of computer screens and hardware before us.) I always try to look at it that way.

Are you involved in politics or activism at any level?

Not currently. When I was in Marlboro College, a lot of times I was into gay pride. We would talk about stuff, you know, concerning that. But it was not an all-the-time thing. Initially, when I got there, they used to joke about the one gay on the campus, and that's pretty much what it was. By the time I left, it was, like, the gay-friendly school to go to. I think it was listed—I can't remember if it was in the *Princeton Review*—but there was a publication that stated the top ten most gay-friendly schools in the country, and Marlboro was right up there.

Pretty much on campus everyone knew who everyone was, everyone knew who was either gay, bi, whatever. The general attitude was if you went there and your attitude wasn't a gay-friendly attitude, typically, you didn't last there. The people that I knew I could go behind them and hug them and they were like, "Okay, Nate," and think nothing of it.

Half the administration was gay and lesbian. By the time I left, the new dean of students, he was gay. We all thought it was so hilarious. It wasn't so much like Marlboro was a gay school or anything. But the community atmosphere it tried to embody, the whole environment and the people it drew in, that helped further the accepting of everyone, though every now and then the argument would come out—we accept everyone, except people who are Republican. We'd laugh about it and realize half the people in the room were Republican.

Were you involved in gay issues before you went to college?

I wasn't out until I went to college. I chose not to be. I knew what

Colombian Red-Tail Boa

kind of bullshit people put up with in high school. So I said, I'll just stay
concealed here; I didn't really have to hide much. Then, when I got in
college, that's when I just kind of stuck my foot in the water. At first I told
people I was bi. When I realized everybody's reaction was, "That's cool,
whatever," then I was gay.

That was the first couple of days. I remember the room I was sitting
in, and the dorm I was in, and the people who were sitting with me. The
funniest part was when there was an article about me [in the *St. Albans
Messenger*]. It was in my senior year in college. I was home on vacation and
this friend sent me an article that some person had wrote about Outright.
I thought, this person has got to be the most ignorant idiot I had met in
a while, even though I had never met them. I decided that rather than
writing some nasty, retaliative letter, I'd write an informative letter. So
I wrote into the *Messenger* and told them all the things I thought about
it, without attacking the person because everybody has the right to their

own opinion. But when they start to throw their opinion at something, as though it should be law, that's when I start having a problem with it.

Was this person taking some kind of anti-gay Biblical stand?

I don't remember if it was Biblical. It ran somewhere along the lines of when people say, "Oh, giving kids condoms makes them have sex more," as opposed to, "If they do have sex, they'll be protected." It was something along that sort of mentality. So I just wrote a frank letter about what I thought about the opinions and a little about what I experienced. It prompted the reporter Leon Thompson to contact me. They did the interview. They took pictures. My partner Mikie was there. I went to grab the paper one day and a friend of mine said, "It's on the front page!" So I went in the store and bought one. And then I found it. To my surprise, my picture was the entire front page, the article was attached to it. I was like, "Holy crap!" I don't remember getting any shit from anyone after that. I think people kind of thought, He's got balls and I better not mess with him.

Now you're back in St. Albans, who makes up your community?

In St. Albans all my friends are gay, or they're work friends, or they're neighbors. I have a very supportive family. An accepting family. Everyone, [even] my grandparents, everyone knew I was gay. It was never really an issue. I didn't think I had to run away to another state, another town. A lot of friends I have who are gay, they just decide, "I have to get away from here." So they go to Burlington. That's like the closest faraway place they can think of. They can be immersed. Plus they're close to bars and clubs. I don't drink. I go to clubs now and then, but more for dancing than anything.

So it's been pretty comfortable being in St. Albans and Franklin County? You don't get hassled because you're gay.

I really don't. Part of it has to do with if you see me across the street, it may not even cross your mind I'm gay. Then there are people who say, "I saw you a mile away and I knew you were gay," and I go, "Whatever." I mean, that doesn't mean that I haven't, occasionally, in my entire lifetime, heard comments here and there. I think that my partner gets more comments than I do because he looks more flamboyantly gay than I do.

Are you more of an intellectual, physical, or emotional person?

Probably intellectual would be the top one. I consider myself kind of like, you know, one wrapped in another wrapped in another. It's almost like a hierarchy. It's almost those are three different parts of myself. One controls another which controls another. Umm . . . what do you mean by physical?

You would go snowboarding and swimming . . . skate boarding. Physical things would have a high priority in your agenda.

I would, yeah, still say my intellectual one is the highest. Physical and emotional are about the same level. The difference is, and I struggle with this with some people, a lot of people think because I don't show my emotion in the utmost . . . in an over dramatic sort of way. If there's something happening that is really hurting me, a relative dies or something like that, if I'm not crying, sobbing, bawling my eyes out, it doesn't mean I'm not feeling it. It just means that's not my physical reaction to it. It's hard when I'm around people who frickin' spill something and they start crying. Then it's like my intellectual side says, That's a little ridiculous; but they can do that, if they want.

(More than anyone else I've interviewed, Nathan really chews over this tripartite division in himself. In a round about way he tells me that he's never emotional before his intellect gives the go ahead, assuring him that such a response is all right.)

It's okay to have the emotion when it's appropriate. If you're in a crisis, that's not the time to get emotional. It's time to think, kick in, to react. Then, after the act, you process it and you can get emotional, if you want. When there's relationship stuff involved, and you need to get emotional, that's fine, as long as the person isn't in the middle of trying to kill themself. . . . (He laughs nervously, thumbs rubbing against each other in his lap.) I'm trying to think . . . the only two times I've gotten particularly emotional in the last, you know, however long I can remember, is one, when my grandmother died. It wasn't so much that I got emotional right off, but I got the phone call . . . it was, like, Mim-may passed away last night. What ended up happening was my intellectual side kicked in in terms of, you know, I need to get up, I need to get dressed, I need to go over there. And even on the way over I'm telling myself, When I walk into that room I'm going to cry because it's going to be sad. It doesn't mean I'm going to hold back, it doesn't mean I should be crying now. It was like, once I got in the room, yup, crying . . . and part of it was crying, part of it was holding back a little just to comfort my mother. It was kind

of a conflict . . . emotional didn't completely take over, but it almost did. The only other time is when relationship stuff starts happening. I sometimes wonder if my partner is a little bi-polar; he'll go into modes where he doesn't realize what he's doing or saying. I've never been, like, beat by him or anything, but some things he'll say, I'll just snap and I just start crying. I know it's not like me to do that, and I know it's a situation that's not a normal situation.

You grew up in Highgate . . . is that an Abenaki town? Are you Abenaki at all?

Not that I'm aware of. My Mim-may was originally from Canada. My Pip-pay, I'm not sure. But I don't think any of my relatives, those close in my blood line, are Abenaki.

We grew up in East Highgate, which is pretty much like in Sheldon. So we didn't grow up in a specific town so much. I had some friends on my road, but I lived on a dead-end dirt road. So the few friends I had were like neighbors down the road. One of them I kept through middle school. I was the loner, kind of, in high school. I didn't really fit with a particular group. I was just there. Whoever I happened to be hanging out with at the time, I was hanging out with. I definitely was not involved with jocks or cheerleaders or whatnot.

Are you a Vermont history buff?

Not really. History and writing are things I never focused on. Now I can do something like watch the History Channel and watch the history of something. But it doesn't hold my interest like something about science does.

If you were to give me an executive summary of the last ten years in the life of Nathan Chates, what would you say?

My executive summary would consist of where I went to school and where I worked. I probably wouldn't even include much of high school. I went through high school, I did a lot of volunteering. I moved on to college, basically, kind of on chance. I got this brochure from this Marlboro College. What is this? I checked it out and loved it immediately. I spent four years in college, and if nothing else, I graduated and I have a degree. That college was good for me to become more of who I am. It helped me become less introverted, more outgoing. More confident. More able to meet people and enjoy going into a new group of people. I love that. It's a chance to interact with new people, get to know new people. I always look at people in a kind of evaluative way. I kind of try to figure them out. Not that I have to figure them out, but it's just kind of fun to figure out how people work, how people tick.

Did you get financial aid for college?

Oh, lots of financial aid. I made it out with like seventeen thousand in loans, which isn't bad, for a thirty-to-forty thousand dollar a year college.

What's your vision for the future? What would you like to see happen?

Actually I've been asked that question before. I'm not doing what I went to college for. I have no desire to be someone who jumps right from college into this high professional crap. I'd rather work my way up because I know, from how I've worked my way up, I appreciate money more, I appreciate life more, I appreciate little things. People I know who have had stuff handed to them, or have just been given jobs, when the real world hits them and you aren't backed up, you start to realize how difficult it is to find work. So I find by taking myself slowly, working up to the career I want . . . I'm only twenty-four . . . it's not very old, even though some people think it is—you know, people who are in high school, "Oh twenty-five, it's so old!" But the way I look at it, there's nothing completely horrid about me taking the next three to four years . . . planning something else financially, which I've done. I work a second job, not because I have to, but I knew my loans and car would take X amount of dollars.

I realize by the time I'm thirty, maybe I won't have a gigantic home but at least a double-wide. I love how double-wides and trailers get the stigma of being trash, but only because a lot of people who live in those don't take care of them. But I've been in lots of trailers and double-wides that look a lot nicer than homes of people I visit.

Do you ever foresee owning your own business?

I've gotten to the point that whoever you work with, you're going to have to deal with stuff. All kinds of issues. I've discovered that working at Staples the issue of money, as a computer technician, is always there. Though I work thirty-seven-and-a-half hours a week, I'm technically part-time. I'm making ten dollars an hour take-home. This is the first job I've planned on leaving because of the way the store is run. The health benefits completely suck. After going in and having one CAT scan, period, and after the insurance paid, I still owed three to four grand. Wow, I thought, that's not good! There's also the fact the hours are so fluctuating. With the fluctuating hours, I hardly have time to do anything. You have to schedule in time to be with your partner.

I like helping people with computers, I really do. But the setting I have to do it in now is not conducive to my way of teaching. You have to worry if you're selling enough, if you're doing that, if you're doing this. And if someone is completely, outright belligerent to you, you can't say a frickin' thing! I would like to be able to say something to them, so that person knows they can't do this. That's one of many reasons I might leave Staples. My hands there are *so* tied, it isn't funny.

What would you like to see happen in Vermont in the next five to ten years?

I'd like to see people in various positions throughout the entire state start to take a hard look at why they're making decisions that are being made. What's really behind it? Take a more logical perspective, rather than "I want it this way, and I'm just going to come up with every reason I can because I want it that way." Instead of saying, "Okay, this should work. This is why it should work, here's the reasons." Take a more logical standpoint, which it doesn't seem sometimes they're doing.

I've got to ask you my four basics.

The four basics?

Yeah. Have you ever milked a cow?

Sort of . . . yes . . . kind of. Meaning my grandparents had a small farm, small being sixty to eighty cows. When we were growing up, they did have milking machines. They had two kinds. They had the carry-around-the-bucket, hook-it-into-the thing. Then, towards the end, they had the one with a big pipe that went along, you hooked up to that. There was one time I decided to just hand milk one day . . . just to see. And, so, yeah . . . (He laughs, thumbs twirling.)

You tapped maple trees?

Definitely. When I was in school we did that sort of thing.

Ever put food by, ever can beets, carrots?

I haven't. Our family was never much of a canning family. My step-mother was more of a canning-sort of person.

How about hunting and fishing?

I've done both. I haven't been lately, I have not had the time. I used to hunt. I definitely went the first year I could. I bagged a fifty-pound button buck which I ended up winning a prize for, for smallest deer, which they didn't tell anybody they were doing because they didn't want people to shoot the smallest deer. Basically, you can feel the nubs, but not really antlers. They didn't tell people there was a prize for the smallest, but I definitely got it. I must have been fifteen or sixteen. It was around the time I could only go youth hunting. We sat up in the hay barn at my father's friend's place. I looked out into a field. Of course, the funny thing was the whole time was pretty much my father and I falling asleep, off and on, throughout the whole day. I'd fall asleep, he'd wake me up; he'd fall asleep, I'd wake him up. Yeah, I sat up there on the hay dressed in six hundred layers of clothing, not being able to move.

Did you shoot your button buck out of the hay loft?

That one wasn't too bad of a shot. I think it was an eighty-yard shot.

And fishing?

I don't have my own fishing pole. I just haven't picked up one or had the money to pay for a license. When we were younger, typically we'd go to rivers, fish in the rivers. Occasionally, we'd go bullpout fishing, which was a lot of fun. It wasn't so much you were actively fishing, but you're kind of all sitting around the fire with the poles all there, the clothespins all hanging from your line, just waiting for it to jump. And it's night. And you're just there, staring at the fire. But it just got to the point where there weren't so many fish biting any more.

A couple of cultural questions. Are you a movie fan, music fan? You read?

I don't do books so much. Something about high school, the way it was all run turned me off of reading, which I probably will pick up again at some point. But, you know, I went to a college that focused on writing and reading. It's kind of ironic. I'm more into TV, but not so much. I don't watch aimlessly. And I've always been a cartoon fanatic. A lot of people, I think, still have the mindset—I think of my parents' generation—the mindset that cartoons are for kids. Very few cartoons are for kids! I was never a comic-book buying person. Part of it was just not having the money to buy comic books. Plus, I can't think of a place I might have bought them when I was younger. I mean, when we were little, if we made a trip to Burlington, that was like people's trips to California, you know.

Music? I can listen to everything. The eighties, heavy metal, pop. Every now and then some rap. Some country. Some whatever. Most classical or most jazz I don't like. But there are ones here and there that I do.

Do you use social media much?

Facebook I use off and on. The funny part is, when my father was in Iraq, he had Facebook. Suddenly, he added me one day, and I added him. The next thing you know, every frickin' relative I had, old and young, is all on Facebook. I was like, Wow, this is not just an addiction for kids! This is also a way to find people you didn't even know anymore, to contact people, a relative or someone who's not near by. I miss my friends from college. Some of them live in California, some in Massachusetts, some live in Ohio. But ultimately, if they're really my friends, they're not going to stop being my friends because I don't live close to them anymore. It's all this communication back and forth. ▪

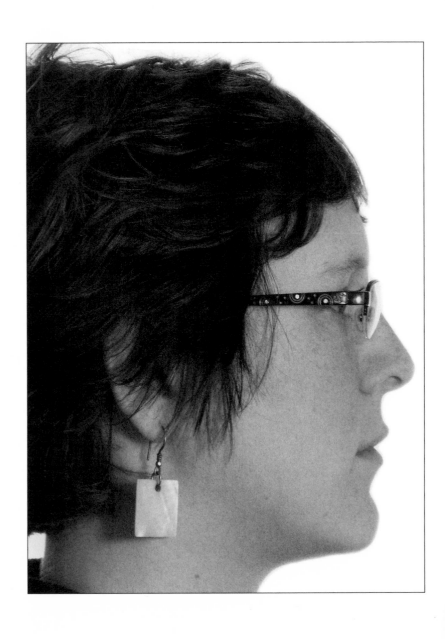

I'm totally dependent on the people around me

Liana Hebb

Born: April 14, 1982
Where: Post Mills, VT
College: Smith College, the Sorbonne in Paris
Degree: Double major: anthropology and French
Married: No
Job: Farm manager

> I find Liana Hebb at the Mountain School, up in the hills of Vershire where she lives in a renovated old schoolhouse. She manages the Mountain School Farm, which produces eighty percent of the food for the forty-five students and fifteen full-time faculty, and is in the thick of the local-foods movement. Well traveled, Liana tells me that she studied French in Paris, did translation and video work in Switzerland, and spent a life-changing year in Vietnam, teaching English to hundreds of students from seven to seventy. "For me, it was a place of deconstruction of my preconceptions and ideas of what was right and wrong and necessary." What was right and necessary for Liana Hebb, she learned, was to return to Vermont, get her hands in the dirt, and make things happen in local-food production and education. She says:

In 2005, the year after I graduated from college, I headed out in September for Saigon. I signed myself up for this training course to become certified teaching English as a foreign language, so I could get a job. After being there for one month, I had to get out of Saigon. I went north to Haifong, a port city directly east of Hanoi. It was really, really difficult. I was isolated culturally, linguistically, in every way. I had to communicate and sustain myself. What I learned was not that I could be totally independent and self-reliant; it was that I'm totally dependent on all the people around me.

The community was amazing. I had five hundred students from ages seven—little kids learning ABCs—up to sixty-year old men who were the proprietors of large industrial plants in an industrial city. But the majority of my students were college students, around my age, so we became friends. They were my teachers as much as I was their teacher. It was difficult because I got stuck living in a hotel for three months, and I had a lot of unforeseen—how could I foresee what I had gone there to discover? My own self-reliance was kind of flipped on its head. That was an awakening for me, but emotionally, I ended up kind of shutting down and just trying to plod along, day by day—out of loneliness, partially.

So Vietnam was a low point for you but with invaluable lessons?

Absolutely.

What was your high point over the last decade?

I have to say that I am so thrilled to be here right now. This whole Mountain School situation just sort of fell into my lap; it's more than I could dream of. It's my . . . it's my ideal job. That's not to say that it's perfect. It's just an incredible opportunity. I have a huge playground and an unlimited scope of creativity and help and young families that live on campus. [There is] also my greater community in the Upper Valley and the Pompanoosuc Agricultural Society [headquartered in Thetford]. Things have started to come together. I've started to feel like, Okay!

For a period I was worried about coming back to Vermont and not being able to find a job. But I knew this is where I wanted to be. I recognized how wonderful I feel in this place. So what I wanted to do was contribute whatever I could to building Vermont's economy for young people in the job market.

Does it feel that Vermont has opportunities and you're plying one of them?

It does to me. Particularly in regards to local food production, as well as other cottage industries and building sustainable communities. That's what I've been working towards with my larger community here, in Thetford, and in the Upper Valley.

Can you describe this community you're talking about?

The people already involved in the local food system are my closest collaborators. The Pompanoosuc Agricultural Society is an organization we founded a couple years ago with a number of residents from Thetford and the surrounding area. It's not entirely in Vermont. We're co-joined with the North Country Farming Association, which is a little north of us and encompasses the Northeast Kingdom and reaches down into Orange County.

What's your role in this community?

Producer and educator in agriculture. I consider myself a facilitator of conversations and, I guess, outreach in that respect. The Pompanoosuc Agricultural Society is not a very bureaucratic organization. We don't have any legal status, but there are fifteen to twenty people from all walks of life involved. The common interest is homesteading and gardening and producing our own sustainable food system. We have people who are retired; we have people just out of college; we have community members; we have the nurse at the elementary school who is coordinating the garden they have there; we have farmers.

Within this state and within this region, most of the farmers on the commercial scale are all very strongly connected [to one another.] Everyone who is marketing to the restaurants and the food co-ops in the area—those producers, I know all of them very well. The central clearing house is Vital Communities, an organization based in White River. It has a large database on where the local food suppliers are, what they produce, and how to obtain their products. It also helps the producers by doing a little marketing. Other than that, it's farmers' markets, it's food co-ops. One of the objectives of the Pompanoosuc Agricultural Society is to form a network of producers that are more on the homesteading scale, as opposed to the commercial scale. Linking people together who want to find fresh eggs . . . or fresh raw milk.

Are the people you're describing retreating from a world they don't like and think should be changed, or are they creating a new world? What's the psychological dynamic?

I think it's a very positive look inward and trying to focus more on sustaining our own communities rather than being reliant on large-scale industrial production for our needs and our food. We are really trying to focus on what we can do ourselves. But it's positive! I mean, in White River Junction, for example, there's this transition town movement, which is also happening in multiple other locations. It's focused on building self-reliant communities, independent of fossil fuels in every respect, from transportation to energy to food to health. It's a movement I feel has a lot of momentum.

What's your background?

My father is a fourth-generation Vermonter. He was born on Thetford Hill, grew up in Thetford. My mother was born in Connecticut, grew up there and in Kentucky. Dad went to Beloit College, and he and mom met in Eugene, Oregon, where they both were working on farms. Eventually, they hitch-hiked across the country back to Vermont, where they set up a shop in Thetford. Now he's an energy consultant. Mom worked for years in early childhood education. Currently, she works in the bakery at King Arthur Flour [in Norwich, Vermont].

How did you, with this background and a degree from Smith and a year studying French at the Sorbonne, end up in the local food nexus?

I've always had an interesting relationship with food that is somewhat unusual because I was raised a vegetarian. The times I've eaten meat in my life I can count, you know, on three fingers. There are incidences when I've eaten it accidentally or at a pot luck. Actually, one time, intentionally, I tried a bite of something. But I have kind of a psychological block against meat—not because I think it would taste bad, but just because, to me, it's not really food. It's . . . it's . . . it's body parts. (She laughs.) Meat's just not my thing. It's not in my lexicon. Even though I understand that meat is delicious and nourishing, and it can be consumed in ways that I consider sustainable—and I don't have any ethical dilemma with animals dying—I just personally can't bring myself to chew and swallow it.

So [my life so far] has always been framed by the vegetarian lens. I've been involved in farming since I was fourteen, working as a high-school student on a summer job. I learned to cook very early; I've always loved to cook. In my family we cooked meals three times a week—each of us traded. All of these things kind of came together when I realized I wanted to be in Vermont and be involved with the land and agriculture. Then the education piece tied into it all when I decided that I really wanted to contribute to the community here.

Are you involved in Vermont politics?

I haven't done any campaigning. I certainly vote and I read. And I consider my purchasing to be a political act, so I try to keep my money in the local economy, that's a political decision for me. I don't do anything more formal than that.

Do a lot of the people who favor a local economy have the same attitude? That is, are they interested in and follow politics, but are not directly involved?

There's a spectrum of involvement. We've had direct discussions with our state representatives, we've gone to hearings on bills affecting farmers. The Democrats have been the most receptive to talking about how to keep government interference out of direct commercial interactions between consumer and producer. That's the issue that's most important to us. It's a conservative idea. A mutual, consensual law would be great to have established, the buyer consenting or agreeing to trust the producer. Then there would be no liability laid on the producer, whereas now, a lot of the regulations coming down from the USDA [United States Department of

Mountain School

Agriculture] are really scary and can run the small farmers totally under. This top-down system of trying to regulate and regulate and regulate more and more strictly, it's devastating and ineffective.

It already is a big issue, especially in meat and dairy. I mean, we don't produce our own dairy here at the Mountain School, and I really wish we could. Our cafeteria is certified under state and federal regulations as a restaurant, and therefore, it can't serve our milk. It can't serve our products that have not been pasteurized. And a pasteurization facility would cost so much. That kind of thing really doesn't guarantee food safety in the least. It's this one size fits all approach. Ultimately, it takes the responsibility off the individual to have a direct connection to their food, or at least have knowledge of how it was produced and feel confident about it. It's just, you know, "Somebody else is at fault if I get sick."

Are you more of an intellectual, physical, or emotional kind of person?

Oh, how do I separate them? (Big smile.) I don't. I try not to. I try to find something that feels satisfying in all three of those realms. That has been a challenge and it's kind of a fleeting balance. I tried office work for one year—I worked at the Pentangle Council of the Art as the administrative manager—and I just couldn't stand sitting in front of the computer. You know, this vein that I've pursued has felt the most rewarding so far because it's intellectual in the education aspect and in learning how to produce food in the most holistic way possible. I'm continually studying, taking courses on nutrient-dense food production and how to manage soil. Then I'm working outside and doing hard manual labor, which I end up loving. And it actually has a spiritual aspect for me. It's very meditative and I find it therapeutic to just, you know, focus on being physical. Of course, that ties into yoga too. [Liana teaches a yoga course in her schoolhouse.] You don't just think about being in your body, and ultimately, you stop thinking . . . just exist.

Does your job demand that you bring your full skill set to it? Not just your brain and your body, but emotions, spirit, everything?

Absolutely. And especially here.

One of the things that has always amazed me about educated people is that so few of us achieve that. You go to Smith, you go to community college, whatever, and then you find a job that wants you to forget much of what you've learned because if you're too humanistic you're going to be in trouble on the job. Or too holistic or too compassionate. Same problem. Now the idea that agriculture, which seemed a kind of a dead-end place for the last twenty or thirty years, is pushing the skills envelope—that's amazing.

Well, there is certainly a stereotype of us being uneducated eighth-grade dropouts who are growing your food.

Yet it's becoming a very satisfying field in which to work.

For me, working on farms through high school was a great job. I loved being in the fields, and I loved getting a tan and having a lot of fresh vegetables. But it really didn't go beyond that. My appreciation has grown as I've integrated myself into the ideas and values of the local food system, and it's a wonderful time to be in this field.

Is Vermont the place people come to to try to learn more about creating local food networks? Are we in the forefront there?

I think so. Not that I have direct experience with out-of-staters saying, "We want to learn how to do this." But within this area there are pioneers in so many respects. I mean, it's happening in Hardwick, it's happening here. It's happening in White River. It's happening in Rutland. Actually, Rutland has an organization called Raffle; it's supporting incoming new farmers.

There's a national organization that is called The Greenhorns. It supports young farmers all across the country, and they've made a nice documentary on that. But here the movement is happening in larger numbers, with more momentum. I think if you look at the per capita numbers in terms of consumption of local foods or farmers markets, Vermont is absolutely in the lead. Which is sort of astonishing to me, given that California can produce food all year around, more easily. But it's on an industrial scale and it's a different kind of system.

Are you a Vermont history buff?

I'm not a buff. I did grow up next to the mill in Post Mills, which is now this dilapidated, falling-down building, and I am very interested in that. I have a visual appreciation of history. I love the stone walls when I'm hiking in the woods. I also have a real appreciation for the old rundown brick industrial complex type of buildings that are sort of scattered throughout the state. I feel almost guilty because I love to look at these buildings . . . I just find them *so* beautiful.

It's also been cool learning how the town of Vershire was started. I believe it was members of George Washington's army who, upon finishing their service in the war, were paid in plots of land in Vershire. However, it was a group of people down in Massachusetts who just divided up the land on a little map. They drew rectangular parcels, having no idea of the lay of the land. Somebody got a cliff, and somebody got a stream. They drew this road straight through the middle, right across this land. It's been really fascinating to think how that affected things.

My standard Vermont questions: Have you ever milked a cow?

Oh, yeah.

You ever made maple syrup?

We used to do that on a very small scale with my parents when I was young. Just boiling on a kitchen stove. Here at the Mountain School we have a beautiful system. We have dumping stations throughout the woods, so the students get to have the bucket experience but don't have to schlep everything down to the sugarhouse.

How about canning?

That's something I really enjoy. I remember apple sauce and dilly beans and pickles when I was younger. Here at the school, we produce eighty percent of the food and the majority of it is grown during the summer.

I'll hire a crew of six to run the farm with me while the students are gone. We'll be harvesting and putting up vegetables.

How do the school cooks take to putting up food?

They love it. One of them comes in whenever we need help. We have a harvest kitchen in the main kitchen.

You hunt or fish?

Being a vegetarian, that wasn't part of my paradigm.

What about winter sports?

I started out [skiing] down hill when I was about three or four, cross-country when I was a little older, and in high school I switched to telemark skiing. I found it so freeing compared to the lock down heels of down hill. Whenever I've had a free day during winter or summer for the past number of years, I've normally just headed out for a hike. Last year I did seventeen mountains over four thousand feet, in the White Mountains mostly.

You don't have an elliptical machine, do you?

No. The previous farm manager here, when I visited, she had an elliptical. She had a big one up in the bedroom.

Let's talk about the future. What would you like to see happen in the next five or ten years? What do you fear happening?

I would really like to see the establishment of more connections between the young people who want to farm and landowners who have prime agricultural land available. In conjunction with that, I'd like to see the creation of more infrastructure in communities to support production and storage, like a community root cellar.

What would a community root cellar look like? Would it be like a huge gym underground?

Yeah . . . sure. (She laughs.) You know, there are low-cost options that you can throw together pretty quickly which involve taking an old container, like a train car or a shipping container, lining it with insulation and spray foam, and installing a cooling element which, of, course, is less sustainable than digging into the ground and using the ambient temperature of the soil. That kind of thing can be thrown together for about five thousand dollars. On the other hand, if we're going to look for a longer term, larger investment, it would be dug and made a big underground facility with separate rooms at different humidity levels and temperatures to really maintain the separation between your apples, carrots, etc.

It'd be good to have a commercial hub of some sort where cottage industries could be housed. Have a retail outlet for local food year around. All these things coming together would make it possible for us to really sustain ourselves.

What do you worry about that may make your local food dreams impossible?

The regulations. The top-down, one-size-fits-all approach that I mentioned before. Proponents of small, independent local agriculture talk about relationships between producer and consumer that are direct and have no middle man. But, you know, we're at real risk of losing our autonomy and our ability to produce and sell anything on a small scale. Particularly, with dairy and meat . . . things can be really nerve-racking. And the same is happening in vegetable production. There's one system called GAPS (Good Agricultural Practices). The USDA is riding it. It's not mandatory yet, but it's getting there. It's sort of consumer driven; it's overwhelming for small farmers just to hire the personnel to keep the records. You have to have a port-a-potty you can take to your fields, and it just goes on and on and on. I mean, this kind of thing has people really worried.

What do you do culturally?

I grew up singing classical music as a family in four-part harmony. I'm currently in the Thetford Chamber Singers. I'm really big into dancing. I've done swing dancing, salsa, ball-room, Latin. I did a lot of what's called international folk dancing: Hungarian, Macedonian, Yugoslavian. Now I'm spending a lot of the time, three or four hours a week, practicing West Coast swing with a group. We're starting to do some performances and some competitions . . . but I don't know about that.

What about social media?

I went through a very short period spending all my time on Facebook. A short, three-day craze. Now I'm very inactive. I do use email, but I try to stay away from that stuff. I grew up with no TV, and that's an important part of my life, to stay away from TV. I find that mainstream culture is just trash. I can't stand it. I avoid it at all costs. I would be happy if I never owned a TV in my life. Although, I like movies. No cell phone. No iPod applications.

The school does use email on campus, and we have Internet accessibility, but it's very limited. There's no cell phone service here. There are no

TVs on campus, and students are really discouraged from that because it takes away from building community life here.

Do you have a favorite quote?

I don't have a favorite quote. But I very much try to live by Eleanor Roosevelt's, "Do something every day that scares you; try to go out on a limb." ■

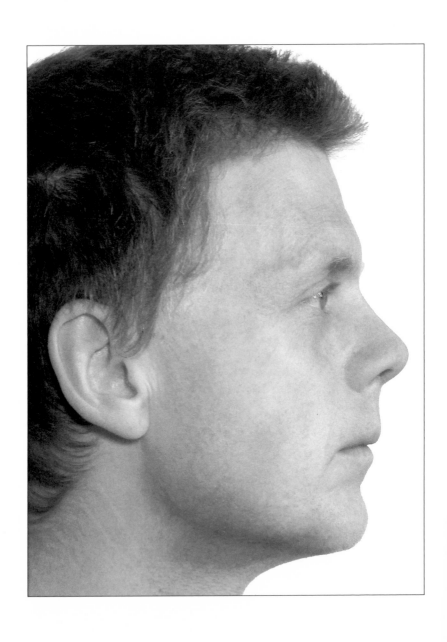

I only shoot animals I love

Ben Hewitt

Born: November 23, 1971
Where: St. Albans, VT
Siblings: One sister, younger
College: Johnson State College
Degree: No
Married: Yes, two kids
Job: Writer and off-grid homesteader; author of *The Town That Food Saved*

Ben Hewitt bought land in Cabot in 1997 and built a shack. The next year he and his wife Penny moved in. Now he calls their place "a classic little subsistence hill farm; it's got just what we need and nothing more." I find Ben in the rough-hewn house, the latest rendition of the original shack, on a grayish winter day not long before the launch of his new book, *The Town That Food Saved*, about the local-food movement Mecca of Hardwick. A lanky man with close-cropped hair, he makes me a coffee and talks briefly about his animals, which live close by in a variety of small structures. For a guy who says, "I spend an awful lot of time playing in the woods and livin' with my critters," and also lives off the grid and out of sight of any neighbors, Ben proves extremely loquacious and, not very surprisingly, very independent.

Let's talk about the economy. How is it affecting your life?

Well, in order to give you a good answer to that, I have to back up a little bit and talk about the way we structured our lives. Both my wife Penny and my goal is to live as frugally as possible, while still having the comforts and the conveniences that a lot of us were raised with and have come to take for granted. Because we built a house basically out of pocket, with most of our own labor and with some help from our friends, and we drive a car that we bought for eight hundred dollars, and we're very committed to living a life fiscally on our terms as much as possible, and since I don't make much freakin' money, the only way we can do that is to keep our expenses to a bare minimum.

Around here, I think there are a lot of people in our shoes. They haven't lived beyond their means. We live still in a rural part of Vermont where people are much more accustomed to just sort of getting by and making do. Maybe some of it is just hidden; I haven't seen the hurt yet in this community. But I'm not a real optimist when it comes to what's coming down the pike. I'm not really buying this recovery. I think we're all going to feel the impact at some point or another.

But the upside of all this is you have a new book coming out. How'd that happen?

The Hardwick book evolved because living here in Cabot I'm a stone's throw from Hardwick. I knew some of the players in Hardwick's agricultural economy, and I became aware that there was something going on that is really interesting. I had never really considered doing a book. I'd kind of trained myself to do magazine stuff. A book always felt sort of intimidating. Too much commitment. All of a sudden it was in my lap and it just felt like, Wow!

Are you pleased with what you've produced?

Yeah, but that's a loaded question. Here's the thing: At first, I thought it was going to be really a great advantage and be really easy to write a book about a town that's just down the road. Then I became aware of how problematic a thing that is. It really forces you into a place of self-editing because you want to be sensitive to these people. If you're coming to a place and leaving a week later, really, who gives a shit what you write about? That's flip, but it's a lot easier to come in and leave and not have to look back over your shoulder. I couldn't do that with this. I wanted to make sure that I wrote a book that I could stand behind with a certain level of integrity and say, you know, "I put in the hours and time really thinking about this." This was the most honest portrayal I could put onto paper and I feel good about that.

Who makes up your community here in Cabot? Do you go to church?

(Flashes half a smile.) No, we don't go to church. We've been here for twelve years [but] it's only in the last six that we really felt integrated into the community. We're surrounded by generational farmers on either side of us. We have a dairy farm down the road. It's an older fellow and his son farming it right now. And we have another farm up the road, and it's two young men in their twenties farming that and it's their grandparents' farm. Jimmy and Ian [Ackerman] are awesome. They're really amazing guys. They are some of the hardest working . . . they are unbelievable. We have really nice relationships with both of these farms. We raise pigs in the summer and I collect waste milk, so I see those guys regularly. Those are the people that really make me feel grounded in this community.

We also have a collection of friends who have children our kids' age. They're our age, the adults are, and they have, by and large, similar values. Either they keep animals or they keep gardens. You know, a lot of people around here still apply those skills. What we're doing here in terms of a broad swath of America is pretty unusual, but around here it's not that unusual. When it comes to basics—you know, when to put in the firewood, when to plant the lettuce—I think that we in this area have a wealth of knowledge that we probably don't even realize we have, even though, clearly, a lot's been lost. I think that's really hopeful.

In a strange way I feel like I connect more with someone like Jimmy and Ian. They live with animals; they're dairy farmers, but they go and ride snowmobiles and dirt bikes. They're kind of good ole boys, in a way, whereas most of our friends here aren't really. Having grown up in working-class, rural Vermont, I feel a little bit more of a connection with that dynamic than I do sometimes with the other people I know.

Are people curious about how you make a living?

There has, in the past, been an assumption that we're trust funders. It's become more clear that that's not the case. People have seen my work in magazines, so they recognize when I say I'm a writer, I actually am. You know, it's easy to say, "I'm a writer." (Ben chuckles, then laughs.) I think it's an occupation that could be viewed with some degree of suspicion and maybe outright disdain. But the fact that we have a pretty vibrant farm enterprise going on here, particularly in the summer, I think that's clear and people relate to that on some level too.

Could you give me a brief physical description of your farm?

We have forty acres, about ten open and cleared for pasture. We have a hundred blueberry plants. Right now we have three milk cows; they're Devon/Jersey crosses. We've got a bunch of steers that we will beef. We have sheep that we keep for lamb and some wool. Right now we have five ewes and one ram. Every summer we do a bunch of pigs, anywhere from three to six. I collect milk all winter long and freeze it in big drums and I feed that over the summer to the pigs.

Who butchers your pigs?

I do. I prefer not to sell the meat; I'd rather barter it. We usually do a party every year and have a big pig roast.

Do you have chickens?

We have layers. We do meat birds in the summer. Our commitment to land and farming really comes from a place of, This is what's enjoyable to us; this is what feels right to us. We don't have some sort of dogmatic goal of producing eighty percent of our food. It's not to be green or sustainable. It's because this is what feels good to us.

In this region of the Northeast Kingdom, what do you see happening as far as sustainability is concerned? What is positive and what negative?

In my mind, there's a misinterpretation of what sustainability really is. It's a word, a term, that is becoming sort of like "green." To me, it's pretty meaningless. I mean, what is truly sustainable? I don't think there's anything about what's going on right now in our culture that is very sustainable, if you look far enough out. I think there's a lot of hypocrisy, a lot of very superficial, lip-service thinking about what is really sustainable and what we should be doing for the long haul. Hand in hand with that, let's talk about this green thing.

Green has become sort of a way to market the latest hybrid vehicle or the latest fair-trade coffee that is flown up from Costa Rica or wherever. Let's be real. People have a really hard time considering the externalities of what's going on. Is it greener to buy a Prius or is it greener to patch up your Subaru and get another year out of it, even though it gets only half the mileage? The message that you're getting in the media is that you need to rush out and get that Prius as soon as possible. Never mind what the mining for lithium does in Bolivia when they're trying to make those batteries. So much of the toll of many of our systems is externalized. We just don't see that. We've been trained to not see that and allow ourselves not to see that. Maybe it's not that much fun to see it; maybe it's not that much fun to have to see it. We will go to great lengths to preserve the status quo. We've had a very, very comfortable existence for the last eight, nine, ten decades. We've been riding this wave of, like, economic goodness ever since the Great Depression. Clearly, there have been cracks here and there, but by and large, it's been up, up, and away.

What do I see good happening? Regionally I do see a lot of people continuing values that have just sort of run through rural America for many generations. In small town, rural Vermont, and I think, by extension, across much of small town, rural America, people are by and large resilient. They are by and large caring of their neighbors. And they possess, particularly in agrarian communities, a great deal of knowledge that has not been lost. I think that's really, really positive. I don't think we've really

been tested yet. You know, it'll be interesting to see, if we are tested, and presumably we will be, I think we will be, how we will react.

Are there still many working farms in Cabot?

Oh, jeez, there's a lot. It's one of the things I really love about it. I'm trying to think how many farms there are . . . . I'd say there are at least eight. And there's just one that ships to Agri-Mark [a large dairy cooperative], which is where Cabot Cooperative gets their milk. Most of the farms in Cabot aren't selling their milk to Cabot cheese. What happened early on here is that a lot of people recognized the potential of organic. I believe there's only one dairy in Cabot that's not certified organic.

If you were to consider yourself mostly a physical, intellectual, or emotional person, which one would be the driver?

(Chuckles) It's definitely not intellectual. Boy, I'd say it's right down the middle between physical and emotional. It is really important to me to be physical. But I really wear my emotions on my sleeve.

My classic Vermont questions: Obviously, you know how to milk a cow.

Yes, I do . . . by hand! I've never even milked by machine.

How about making maple syrup?

We make a little syrup every year. We did four gallons. We did it on our cookstove, but four gallons is a lot. So I bought a hobby evaporator [used, from Craigslist], just a few months ago. Four gallons on a kitchen stove was too much, it was crazy. I don't wanna do that again. But I love sugaring. It's just *so* fun to, like, go out there and collect the buckets. The whole process is a really nice way to change seasons.

How about canning food? Do you put food by?

We do put a lot of food by. We don't can, though. We do a technique called lacto-fermenting. You can lacto-ferment almost anything. We do carrots. We do green beans, we do peas, you can do just about anything. And we have freezers. We have a root cellar.

You hunt or fish?

You know, I didn't grow up hunting and it's not something I've taken up. We do slaughter most of our own livestock ourselves. So I am familiar with shooting animals, but only ones I've come to love.

Talk to me more about this: I only shoot animals I've come to love. It's something so distant from the way virtually all people live now.

Well, it clearly makes me different. I don't think there are a lot of people in this country who would be willing to kill their own meat. They might, under different circumstances, but if there's an opportunity for them to go down to the store and buy it, they will. You know, I've come full circle to where I'm not willing to go to the store and buy my meat. It became really important for me to actually be part of the slaughter process—not just to raise the animal. You know, it sounds kind of flip: "I only kill animals that I love." But it's not really, it's really true. There's a pragmatic reason to make your animals tame, so that they'll come to you when you slaughter them. It makes them much easier to handle, much easier to slaughter. But it's also, I think, much more respectful of the animal to give it some emotion and to form that bond. You know, it's not always easy. I don't really look forward to slaughtering days.

What about winter sports?

I used to alpine ski a lot because I was an editor at *Skiing* magazine. Now I hardly do any of that any more. I'm not a fan of getting into a car and driving to play. And we have such a great playground out here. We ski around here a lot. A few years ago I bought a Stiga, a specialized steering wheel sled. It's a freakin' rocket. So we sled a lot down this hill and we ski a lot. We don't have a TV, we don't spend a lot of time engaged in passive entertainment. We cut and split all of our own firewood. This time of the year I'm working on next fall's firewood. People around here think that we're crazy because we split our wood by hand. I actually love splitting by hand. My feeling is that if you have good splitting wood and you're splitting on a good cold day, it's as fast as a splitter. You might get a little tired after the first cord and slow down a little bit, but a splitter's no fun. (Ben makes a shrill mechanical noise.) WRAAA! You got to lean over and pick them up . . . I'd just as soon split by hand.

Are you a Vermont history fan?

As I get older, I become more intrigued. My real interest is knowing like what went on on this piece of land. Down in the woods is an old stone foundation from a sugarhouse. I'd just love to know about the lives of the people who worked that. Like everyone else, despite the bucolic nature of the surroundings, I haven't taken the time to really research that stuff.

If you could identify one thing that has happened in Vermont during your lifetime that you could change, what would it be?

(He repeats the question very thoughtfully.) One thing that I could change? I can certainly identify things that I would like to change, but I can't name one thing. I definitely think we have not been supportive enough of agriculture in this state. There has been a lot of lip service. I think that the deconstruction of our railway system is something that we may come to regret. It'd be easy to say that we've been too free and easy with development, but I don't know if that's realistic.

During the last decade what was your low point? What was your high point?

I couldn't really identify either for you. Despite the fact that I have a pretty dim view of certain facets of the American way of life and the future that that suggests, I'm largely an optimist. I mostly spend my days in a pretty damn good mood and feeling a lot of gratitude for the fact that I can get up in the morning, go out and tend to my animals and have that time when the kids come out and go around and do chores with us. You know, as a family we all get dressed together in the morning, go outside and do chores. Even if it's ten below, we all get dressed and do that. And that to me is, you know . . . I just hope I can keep doing that for the rest of my life.

The low point might be last summer. I threw out my back. I've had injuries before from skiing, and I had a cycling accident and broke my collar bone. But I never had one when I was incapacitated. And I was incapacitated. I mean, like, pissing-into-a-Coke-can incapacitated. I couldn't get to

the bathroom. Boy, I don't know what I would have done if I'd had a stroke. It made me sort of aware—I mean it sounds kind of trite because I think everyone has dealt with this on some level or another—but this was sort of an awakening for me to the fragility of my body. I sort of felt—I'm not gonna say that I felt immortal because I'm old enough to recognize that that ain't the case—but it was a certain awareness that it could be taken from me pretty suddenly.

How'd you hurt yourself?

I'd borrowed a wood splitter and I was loading it up. (This triggers my laughing since he just said he didn't like the thing.) I'm serious! I had this big hunkin' piece of beech and I was trying to load it. There was a period there like, "Oh my God, did I slip a disk? Am I going to have to have surgery? What's going on here? What does this mean in my future?" It took a long time, about five days of can't move and then another week of like hobbling around.

Do you have a health insurance?

We do now. We're beneficiaries of the Catamount program (a state-supported health insurance for people of less-than-average-but-not-destitute means).

Do you think your lifestyle is a model for people who might want to try living a different way?

I hate to hold up anything that I do as a model for anyone else because it's somewhat presumptuous. We do things for our own set of criteria and reasoning. One thing I will say that I feel very strongly about is regarding our expectations as consumers and our expectations regarding what conveniences we should have at our fingertips. Relative to most Americans, you know, ours are pretty freakin' low. If there is one thing I get up on my soap box about, that would probably be it. I guess you can't really blame people because they're bombarded by messaging all the time suggesting that everything about them is inadequate: the cars they're driving are inadequate, this and that is inadequate, and the only way to make it adequate is to go out and buy this or that.

We really try to be thoughtful about the purchases we make. We're in year two of the car we've bought for eight hundred dollars, and I'm hoping to get a couple more years out of it. It's not about green or being sustainable or being environmentally friendly. It's sort of a deeper ethic than that, I think. There's a finite amount of resources on this planet, and somewhere someone does not have something that I have. I don't really feel great about that, and I don't want my kids to grow up thinking that just because they were fortunate enough to be born in a country of abundance that they should be able to carry forth and assume and expect that abundance for the remainder of their days. Now, having said that, I'm well aware that our standard of living is higher than probably ninety percent of the people on the globe. But what's important to me, and what I wish I saw more of is people moving in a different direction.

Where would you like to see Vermont going in the next decade?

I think what would be good for the state as a whole is to appreciate more deeply its own resources and to understand that it may not always be in our best interest to be shipping those resources to other places in exchange for money. You know, sort of recognizing that globalization is not an exponential thing. We're just not going to get more and more globalized; in fact, I think we're on the cusp of heading back the other way. For that, Vermont's got a lot going for it. It can care for its own in a lot of ways that other states and other regions can't.

Americans are short termists, in general. It's hard for people to take a long view. It's not politically expedient; you're not rewarded politically for taking a long view, ever. And you're not rewarded fiscally, typically, for taking a long view. So we don't take long views. You know, that's really going to come back to bite us. It's like when the rest of the nation is changing, you feel like, Oh, we're being left behind. So you try to change too, but the reality is you might have actually been way ahead to stay where you were.

A couple cultural questions. Who are your favorite writers?

I've always been a Raymond Carver fan. Poetry, I really like Hayden Carruth. Fiction, T. C. Boyle, I'm a big fan of his. I do read a good bit of nonfiction but at this point in my life, it's fairly rare for me to sit down with a book and really, like, stick to it. So I read a lot of magazines: *The New Yorker, Harpers, Atlantic.* I'm still intellectual enough, I guess, to still enjoy that. I read a lot of anthologies. Every Christmas my mom gives me *The Best American Essays, The Best American Short Stories.*

Do you use social media?

Funny that you should ask. A lot of people are saying, "You've gotta get on Twitter, you've gotta get on Facebook to promote your book." And I'm like, "I don't wanna do it." My feeling is there's going to be a backlash. All we've done is sort of disconnect from each other.

I'll give you an example. I was out in California, working on my next book. I was visiting the largest raw milk dairy in North America. I come out of SFO [San Francisco International Airport] on a little air train in one of those little cars, and there's fourteen of us in this one car. Of those fourteen, nine were doing this. (Ben holds up his hand and wiggles his fingers.) With their Smartphones. Two of the others, women, were actually engaging in conversation and looking at each other. The conversation was about a friend of theirs who had resolved to include the word "beer" in every Facebook posting for 2010. And I was like, Wow, this is where we're going? It's presumptuous of me to think that what I'm doing is any deeper than any of that because, maybe, cosmically, none of it frickin' matters in the least. But I still do feel that way, presumptuous or not. For me it feels more important, and fills me, to live in a place where that's not a part of my experience. I'm sure most people in that car clearly didn't think there was anything weird about what was going on. I felt like I had gone down the rabbit hole. It was just bizarro-land. There's that book by Derek Jensen. It's called *The Culture of Make Believe*. And I think it's a really apt title for where we are in this particular moment in this civilization. ∎

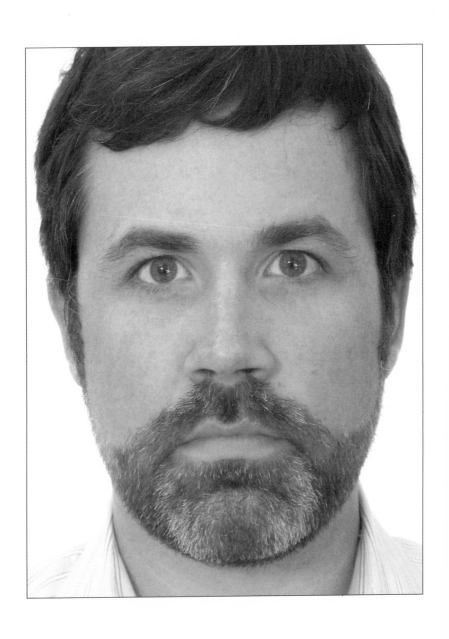

Make it look like a park

Erik Hoekstra

Born: January 11, 1978
Where: Hammond, IN
Siblings: One brother, younger
College: University of Wisconsin
Degree: Double major: Finance & Banking; Real Estate & Urban-land Economics
Married: No
Job: Developer

> Erik Hoekstra's roots are Dutch. His grandfather, who took Erik to
> western Europe when he was fourteen, loved aphorisms, one of which
> stuck in his grandson's mind: "Make it look like a park." That direc-
> tive, combined with an upbringing around Chicago that involved lots
> of moves that stopped in "a great place, an old, turn-of-the-century
> commuter suburb, with a downtown with shops and restaurants and
> great public schools you could walk and ride a bike to," sparked an
> interest in the built landscape at a young age. The interest grew while
> Erik attended the University of Wisconsin, expanded when he worked in
> New York City briefly, then shifted to Vermont after he saw the World
> Trade Towers come down at close range—a memory he recalls when we
> talk at Redstone, his employer in Burlington.

Were you at work that day?

I was about four blocks away when it happened. That had a pretty
profound impact on me, though it didn't have the same impact on me that
it had on a lot of New Yorkers who had friends and relatives and colleagues
that died in the tragedy. I hadn't been there long enough to have a lot of
relationships like that.

What were you doing in New York?

In January 2001 I started a job at CB Richard Ellis, a huge real estate
company, coordinating office renovations and moves. It was a job I was
not passionate about, but I saw it as a stepping stone. While I was there,
I started learning more about urban planning. I got really into New
Urbanism. I read Jane Jacob's book *The Death and Life of Great American
Cities* and really dug into the subject and did a lot of soul searching about
what I wanted to do with my life professionally. The plus side of my job

was I didn't have a lot to do and I had a lot of freedom and nobody really asked questions when I wasn't around.

[After 9/11] it was a bad, bad year. And it didn't look like things were going to pick up in the real near future. I had a friend up in Vermont and I had visited a few times. I was really attracted to Burlington. It reminded me a lot of Madison where I went to school—a progressive university town on a lake, with a vibrant downtown and an old development pattern with density and walkability and pedestrian orientation. My friend offered me her couch for the ski season, and I quit my job and came up to Vermont with very little money and no plan. I got a part-time job, working at Smuggler's Notch. I pieced together some consulting work through contacts I'd made in New York, and things just kind of came together in a very strange and very timely way. In the fall of 2002 I was offered a position at a state-wide non-profit called Housing Vermont, right here in Burlington. Housing Vermont had built something like forty-five hundred affordable apartments all over the state. I got hired into a brand new position they had just created, junior developer. My job was to take projects already committed to and help our local partners make them happen.

Did you do any memorable projects with Housing Vermont?

One is right here in Burlington, down by the skate park on the water-front, called Waterfront Housing. It was the first certified green apartment building in the state. That site was a brown field. People used to drive down Depot Street and throw their couches or refrigerators or whatever over the bank. That bank was just littered with junk. We were not only creating affordable housing but we were cleaning up a brown field and dealing with erosion problems and creating storm water treatment for that whole neighborhood. The project got a prestigious national award for affordable housing built in an environmentally responsible way. I got to go down to a huge green building conference in Atlanta to accept the award on behalf of Housing Vermont in front of a crowd of about twelve thousand people.

The other project I often think about was much different. It was in Groton, on the edge of the Northeast Kingdom. Groton was a very small town with an old village center. There wasn't much happening in Groton any more. The Gilman Housing Trust brought us in to work with the town to acquire four buildings in the village center, including the historic general store. We created nineteen apartments, affordable apartments, a renovated space for a general store, three small spaces for commercial use

Waterfront housing

and a new home for the town library. We put something like four million dollars into the core of this tiny little town in the Kingdom. The impact it had and the experience that I had working on the project for the better part of three years was really neat.

[But] there was a part of me that wanted to get some experience working in the private sector, and the one company that appealed to me was Redstone. These guys weren't doing strip malls, they weren't doing suburban office parks, they weren't doing the kinds of projects that most people think of when they think of commercial real estate development. These guys were doing historic restoration and adaptive reuse of old warehouse buildings. Things to me that were really interesting and creative and exciting. One day I ran into [one of the principals] and he suggested I come meet with him and his partner. They were looking for a junior development person to fill a position that they hadn't even created yet.

How old you were then?

I was twenty-eight. It was an opportunity I might not see again if I didn't jump on it.

And what do you do here now?

Most of the people at Redstone are brokers. I'm the only one in Redstone that works really for the house on behalf of the principals, carrying out projects and acquisitions.

And where are the principals?

They're here. This is it, the Vermont office.

Okay, that was a few years ago. Now we're in a darker economic era. Where do you think this economy is going?

I see two possibilities. One is that we're on a front end of a very slow recovery and things will start to improve. The more cynical side of me sees another wave in the commercial mortgage market that hasn't hit yet. If it hits the way some folks are thinking it will, it can put us in another pretty deep trough for quite a while.

Going back to 2005, there were a lot of securitized mortgages on the commercial side similar to the securitized mortgages that got us in trouble on the residential side. A lot of those mortgages are coming due. This isn't really a Vermont thing; we haven't seen that around here. But in the big city markets there's this potential for a tremendous amount of distress from foreclosures. It could start happening this year. More of it is scheduled in 2011 and 2012.

Why didn't Vermont get swept up in this?

We don't have lots of outside investments coming into Vermont. We don't have aggressive real estate investment trusts and private equity firms buying up commercial real estate. We don't have a lot of office parks; we don't have huge apartment complexes. Most of the commercial stuff is owned locally, and the loans are through local or regional banks. Those banks, for the most part, were comparatively conservative in how they underwrote loans while things were going nuts in other places in the country.

What about your personal experience in Vermont over the last decade? Have you had a high point, a low point?

It's hard to pick one point that's the high point. I guess one, in a series of high points, is when I bought my house in the Old North End in early 2002. It's a Burlington classic, a single-family home chopped into two units. I've lived on the first floor and had different tenants over the last six years upstairs.

Everybody I talked to told me, "You don't wanna live in the Old North End. That's the bad part of the town, there's a lot of crime, it's rough." (Erik laughs.) There was a crazy family living across the street, kind of a classic Old North End family. They sat around in the front yard in the summer, drinking beer, yelling at people all day long. Typical kind of situation.

Directly across the street from them, and right next door to my apartment, was another family that, for the most part, kept to themselves. But occasionally they would come out and get into some altercations with the folks across the street. There were screaming matches. One day I saw the two patriarchs getting into a fist fight. Later it came out that the more subdued family next door to me was dealing heroine. So they lost their home and a young couple bought it and spent a couple years living there and fixing it up. Then they sold it to me. A couple years later, I was able to buy the property across the street where the derelict family lived. I rehabbed that house. There's a really nice professor's family from UVM and his wife and his two small kids living there now.

Do you feel a little guilty being a force of gentrification?

I get asked that question a lot. For any neighborhood or community to be healthy, you have to have a good mix. It can't be all low income people. A nice thing about the Old North End is that the Champlain Housing Trust has been active for twenty-five years and there's a tremendous amount of good, affordable housing that will always be affordable housing. My street's good and it just keeps getting better. With the exception of the drinking, screaming derelicts, nobody's been pushed out from the neighborhood. Everybody else on the street—there are a lot of people on our street that have been there for fifty years, twenty, thirty years—they're good hard-working people. They've been good folks to have around.

Who makes up your community?

When I first moved here, I spent a lot of time hanging out with the radical rebels. But over the years I've gravitated to a group of friends that are more young professional types. For the last few years in the summer time I've played kickball with a big group of folks here in Burlington. We play with a big red ball on a baseball diamond from just after work, like, from 6 o'clock, until the sun goes down. Then we usually have a barbeque. It's co-ed and most teams have between fifteen and twenty people on their roster. I'm the captain of our team. We're the only neighborhood-based team. We call it the Old North End Ballers.

What about the future? What would you like to see happen in Vermont the next few years?

One thing—and it's a topic a lot of people talk about—is the brain drain and the loss of young people in a rapidly aging population where we have an ever-depleting work force. I'd love to see Vermont really figure out how

to begin to tackle those problems, how to begin to keep young people here. Not necessarily to keep *all* young people here. I think it's good for young people to get outside Vermont and experience other places and get some perspective. The high school students that graduate in Vermont and go to school somewhere else often figure out how to come back here eventually and contribute what they've learned outside Vermont to making Vermont a stronger and better place.

Part of the solution is creating interesting job opportunities for people here. To some extent it might be the people we're trying to attract here.

There's a lot of activity in Vermont that's very small scale, entrepreneurial. There's some exciting stuff gaining serious momentum in alternative energy. Companies like Northern Power are shipping the stuff they make to other parts of the country and other parts of the world. I've seen waves of people moving to Vermont from New York, from Boston, and tele-commuting. Really taking jobs from other places and bringing them here and supporting themselves and their families.

And there's another thing I want to mention about the future. One of the things that really frustrates me, living here, is we talk a lot about sustainability in Vermont, we talk a lot about green building and smart growth and anti-sprawl and that kind of stuff. We don't really live it. We don't really do it in practice. Burlington hasn't grown in forty years. While greater Chittenden County grows, and while suburban neighbors like Williston, South Burlington, Colchester, are growing at double-digit percentages, like ten percent a year, Burlington hasn't grown. If we really are the sustainable, smart, growth-oriented, green-building city that we claim to be, we should be growing. That's been incredibly frustrating to me, to be in Burlington and have all the rhetoric and not be able to make smart growth happen here. That's something I'd like to see change, but I'm not sure if I will.

Another problem is, it's incredibly expensive to go to college in Vermont as a Vermonter. It's crazy to me that you can be an eighteen-year old, born and raised in Vermont, graduate from high school here, and it's cheaper for you to go to the University of Wisconsin as an out-of-state student than it is to go to school here at UVM.

Do you consider yourself an intellectual, physical or emotional person?

Somewhere between intellectual and emotional. I'm not a very physical person. I didn't play sports growing up. And the two organized sports, if you want to call them sports, that I play as an adult are kickball and bowling.

My standard Vermont questions: Have you ever milked a cow?

No. I've seen it done. I think I get it.

How about making maple syrup?

I haven't tapped trees. My boss here at Redstone taps trees around his house in Colchester, and boils, just for fun. He has people come and pitch in. He uses buckets.

You ever canned food?

Once. And I was only involved in a small way. I have a plum tree in my backyard that started fruiting last season. This season we've got tons of plums. My girlfriend made jam and I helped her a bit. We boiled the heck out of the fruit and threw in some sugar and some jelly stuff. We've got enough for, I think, three jars.

Do you hunt, fish?

Since I've lived in Vermont, the only fishing I've done is up in Alburg at a lake house. Actually, I caught a fish there. I think it might have been a small-mouth bass, but I'm not positive about that. I did a very little bit of grouse shooting with a friend in northern Minnesota once, but we didn't get anything. My views on hunting have definitely changed since I've lived in Vermont. I grew up with a mother that was anti-hunting. Every deer was Bambi, that sort of view. But I eat meat and it makes sense to me that if you're gonna eat meat why not hunt some of your own meat? So there's a part of me that's kind of interested in hunting and giving that a try.

What's your cultural scene?

I love movies, I definitely enjoy music quite a bit. My music tastes have shifted over the last ten years. In high school I was very into classic rock and got into the Grateful Dead and listened to Phish—that kind of jam band scene. In the last ten years I've gotten more into alternative indie rock. One of the best concerts I've seen in a long time was last fall up in Montreal at Metropolis. The headliner was a band from New York called TV on the Radio. And the opening band, who I now really like and didn't know about, was the Dirty Projectors. They're just kind of funky rock.

Do you use social media a lot, either at work or in your personal life?

A fair amount. I use Facebook but I don't tweet. I've used Facebook to connect with a lot of old friends that I lost touch with, which I think is what a lot of people do. I'm connected to a lot of people that I know in Burlington, so it's a great way to find out about what's going on around the town. Redstone created a fan page on Facebook. So we have fans of Redstone. We use it to spread word about the stuff that we're doing.

Do you have a favorite quote?

Man . . . my grandfather's got a lot of quotes. When I was probably fourteen, my eldest cousin had this sweatshirt made for my grandfather that's got all of his quotes. Some are complete gibberish. They're a hodge-podge of English, Dutch, and Spanish that he learned from farm hands. He's just turned eighty-seven. When he's traveling abroad, all foreign language speakers in his mind are speaking some modified version of Spanish. He uses his own modified version of Spanish to try to talk to people, and people think he's totally nuts.

He's pretty great. He was a failed farmer that got lucky. The Illinois tollway decided to build a highway on his farm. So they bought his farm, and he started a heating oil delivery business in south suburban Chicago, in an area that because of the interstate highway system became a rapidly growing area between the late 1950s and 1980s. My favorite saying of his is, "Make it look like a park." We don't know exactly what it means.

Can you briefly summarize your last ten years in Vermont? Have you become who you hoped to become?

I'm certainly not where I thought I'd be when I was twenty-two-years old. Moving to Vermont, everything that I'd thought that I'd do as a professional, and as an adult, changed. Moving to Vermont was probably the best thing I could have done. I would not have had, even if I'd found a job in New York or some other big city, I wouldn't have had the same breadth of experience that I've had in Vermont. I worked in organizations that are, from the Vermont perspective, big. But from the everywhere-else perspective are very small. I've got incredibly hands-on experience that you typically don't get as a twentysomething or thirtysomething young professional. You usually pigeon hole into a very focused area where you don't see the big picture. I've really had the opportunity to work more like an owner. I've got my hands in a little bit of everything. And it's been a cool experience.

(Erik pauses a minute.) On Friday, I got the letter saying I was accepted into a master's program in real estate development at Columbia. My girlfriend and I are planning to move down to New York. I start a one-year program at Columbia in June. I'll be in the School of Architecture. The program is attractive to me because it's coming from a design and construction focus. I don't know what I'm gonna do after grad school. Coming back to Vermont, to Burlington, is definitely a possibility. I have a house here. I'm not selling my house. I have a lot of connections and ties here that are not going away. ∎

I love it here

Becky Johnston

Born: November 4, 1988
Where: Sherbrooke, Quebec
Siblings: Five brothers, two older, three younger
Married: No
Job: Ski tech in rental shop; bartender

Born and raised outside Sherbrooke, Quebec, Becky Johnston moved to Vermont in 1997, when her parents divorced. She spent her high school years in foster homes in Vermont and Tennessee. A tall, high-spirited young woman, she exudes the confidence of experience gained under those trying years, a confidence not normal for most of her peers with similar histories of living under the roofs of strangers. Wearing a Burton snowboard cap, she comes to my house in Montgomery, where she has just moved into an apartment. We sit by the woodstove and talk.

What do you like about Vermont?

I like that it's small. Almost everywhere you go, it's very community based. It's very relaxing and people aren't rushing around, trying to get anywhere.

I love Montgomery. I love it here—it's great. Having the ski mountain and having such a tight-knit community, where the ski mountain is—you don't see that very often. You always see big towns and all the stuff going on. But there's not much going on here. I like that a lot.

Who makes up your community here?

Like I can't say there's a certain group. I hang out with everybody. There's also my community at the Snowshoe [a bar and lodge where she works in Montgomery Center.] It's family, kids are there, grandkids. All the time. It's safe, it's fun.

What do you not like about living here?

Hmm . . . it's easy to not know what's going on everywhere else. You know, I don't watch television. I've lived in Montgomery Village for about a month now, and I haven't dropped out of town, except to Jay. It kind of keeps you locked here; it's almost a shelter kind of place, in a sense.

What do you want to do with yourself? Any big plans?

That's a good one. I'd like to say I have plans. There are plenty of things

I want to do, but I just don't have a plan. I always let it come and go. Although I would like to probably own a house and have something to do with child and adoptive services.

In 2002 I went into foster care. I was in foster care until 2006. I aged out when I was eighteen. I know a lot and I saw a lot through being in foster care that a lot of people don't see. They go to college and they can have experience, but they don't have the variety of experience that I do. Sometimes I'd sabotage the care; sometimes I let it work. Moving around, I saw a lot of ways that people work.

If you go into child services, what kind of track would you follow?

Well, I've kind of started, in a sense. I do trainings for foster parents. It's only, like, once a month, or every couple months. But when they do trainings, they have guest speakers. And I go in and I speak. All the people are allowed to ask me questions because they're worryin'. You know, they're all fresh out into it, and they don't have any idea. I just answer them, let them know how it was for me—from the eyes of a foster child. I speak from the child's point-of-view.

I still deal with the state a lot. I have a lady who works with me, and we work on things. But it wouldn't take much, if I wanted to do foster care, per se, to start. I would, basically, just have to own a house and fill out some paperwork. It wouldn't be difficult. But to go on, if I wanted to be a social worker, then I'd have to go to school.

When you were in foster care, where did you live?

All over. (She accentuates both words, repeats them.) All over the place. I went to five different high schools. I went to People's Academy, I went to Lamoille Union, Hazen Union. I was in a residential home in Bennington, Vermont, so I went to a school there.

And I spent a summer at a foster home in Tennessee. In Shelbyville, south of Nashville. I liked Nashville.

Now you're here and working (both at the Snowshoe Lodge and at Jay Peak) and we're in a dark, negative economy. Do you get much of a feel for that?

I do. The one place I notice the biggest change is the bar at Jay. The new bar up there—it did wonders. It has done a great, great job. It's always busy. People look like they're really having a good time. It's really nice to have something like that. There's not a whole lot of places you can go here where it's actually a really nice place. When people get done skiing at 4 o'clock, there's nothing to do on the mountain. Sure, they can do a snowshoe tour or go sledding on those red death sleds—but there's *nothing* to do. So by putting in an ice skating rink, by putting in this bowling alley, and all these things [being built as part of Jay Peak's $100 million expansion], it's going to give people on vacation something to do. Though it irritates the locals.

I hear a lot of frustrated people. "Oh, they went ahead and built this hotel—they should expand the mountain. Blah blah blah." It's business, you know. They can't expand the mountain until they expand where they're going to put the people that might come flooding in. They're building one hotel that's family based. Another is—how would you say it—rather hoity-toity. That's where they're putting a water park, behind this hotel.

What kinds of things irritate you?

Lack of common sense; that's a pretty big one on my list. (She laughs.) I don't get irritated . . . that's pretty much it; I'm pretty relaxed in every-thing else. But that common sense and . . . (she laughs again) . . . rain in the wintertime. I was riding up the chairlift yesterday, and I looked down and I saw grass. I was like, You should not be seeing grass in February.

What do you do in your free time?

Snowboard.

Do you feel you're more of a physical, emotional, or intellectual person?

Physical. (No hesitation there.) I'm not really those others. In the summertime I like to do a lot of mountain biking; I'm pretty into that. I'm going to buy a long board and try to get really good at that. I go skydiving. I love swimming, love the water.

Where were you at the start of the decade, in 2000?

In Morrisville, Vermont. After my parents divorced, my mother moved me and my brothers to the town. I didn't like it very much at all. It was really difficult coming from a small, small area, and then being put into a town—well, to me, it was a lot bigger. There was too much going on for me then. I was in school there from 1997 until 2002. I did my senior year at Richford High School [a town next to Montgomery where the town sends some of its high school students]. I got shipped here, to Montgomery, right before my senior year. They put me in a home and I . . . I was *so* mad, and very concerned as to why anybody would live in a town like this. I hated it. I absolutely hated it. But it grew on me.

I lived right down on Route 118, between the village and the center. I got to know people. I really liked the simplicity of it, and the mountain is a key component. You know, the first few years here I didn't have a car. People in New York City don't have a car. And you don't need a car if you live in Montgomery in a sense, either. I just got a ride to work in the morning. And that's what I liked the most. This is my fourth year at Jay Peak. My first year I worked in the kitchen. My second year and third year I was a lift attendant. Then I went to the rental shop, which was last year.

Over this last decade what would you say were your high and low points?

The low point was in 2007. I was pretty lonely. Things just weren't going that well. I hadn't had much contact with my mom and brothers after being in foster care for so long. It was a lot to deal with. So I called my mother and said, "You need to move back here from California. You need to be here." And she came.

The high point, I would say, was the beginning of 2009. It was a very big high point. My family got together a lot. My mother hadn't seen my youngest brother in probably five years. Now she sees him all the time. My mom does housecleaning for herself in Morrisville. My dad, we have a good relationship, but we don't stay in contact as much. He's a long-distance truck driver, so he's on the road. He drives out of Montreal, and he drives all over the United States. I've spent a lot of time on the truck.

My standard Vermont questions: You ever milk a cow?

It's been a while; I might be a little rusty. My uncle had a farm and we used to go up there and he'd let us help him milk.

Ever tap maple trees?

Never.

How about canning?

Nope, I haven't. Not yet.

Hunting and fishing?

I do a lot of fishing in Lake Eden; I use a canoe and catch bass and pumpkinseed fish. A boy I was dating a while ago, he'd take me fishing up around Jay, a lot of time walking around through the woods. I also got my hunting license and did it for one year. I saw plenty but never shot anything.

Let's talk about the future. What would you like to see in your future?

I would like to travel some, see what's out there. I'd like to go to British

Columbia, some place I could ski and ride. I'd probably go to Whistler Mountain, get a ski pass, and stay there. I'd love to be a professional ski bum.

If I didn't find a place that feels as great as this, then I'd come back here and buy a house and live here. It's pretty far fetched at this point. I'd have to get a darn good job. I'd have to save a lot of money

Buying a house is something we should be more knowledgeable about. I couldn't look at a piece of property and tell you, "It's going to run in this range." You're not really educated in that. It's within learning—that's where you should start learning, about houses.

What would you like to see happen here that might help you, make it easier for you to make a decent life for yourself?

I don't want to see too much more development. I'd like to see—it's hard to say less development and more jobs; it's hard, but ideally, what you want. I'd just like to see it pretty much look the same. (She ponders that for a few moments.) Maybe I'm coming to a different perspective about it. If there's an indoor water park and an ice rink at Jay, that means lots of skiers will be off the mountain. They won't ruin it for the locals. The hard thing about change is to realize what it is. There's both good and bad. I'd rather look for the good. I'd rather look for the good (she says with a big smile); always something good comes out of change.

What about politics? Do people your age have much awareness of or interest in politics?

I know a little. Not too much. Actually, not much at all. I'd say in my eighteen-to-twenty-five group, most aren't interested. Once you get past that age, I'd say that's when people start paying more attention to things and caring about things. But between those ages you don't have that much responsibility. You don't. Then you finally start settling down. (Her voice settles down as well.) You start caring about things.

Do you know much about Vermont history?

I know a little bit: covered bridges, the underground railroad thing. I went to a couple of houses where they hid slaves. We used to drive by this place in Wolcott, with connecting houses; there's a path beneath the houses. That's interesting. It always amazes me, when I look at pictures and see horses going down the dirt roads, and Main Street was dirt. I like that.

Culturally, what do you like to do?

I listen to a lot of music. I listen to everything. I get picked on a lot for the kinds of music I like to listen to. The Funkleberries are a big hit with me. I like them. And Sara Grace.

How about computer use? Are you a social networker?

Yeah, I work a lot with the wonderful Internet, Google. I'm a Facebooker. I spend probably four or five hours a day, between personal stuff and work. I did data entry for Mardi Gras at Jay Peak; I was using spread sheets. We have a Wi-fi connection in the house.

Final question: are you worried about the future?

Nope. ∎

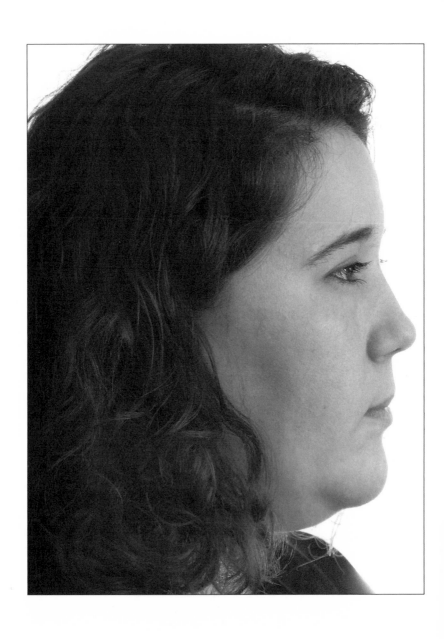

I'm addicted to Facebook

Crystal Lampman

Born: March 13, 1979
Where: St. Albans, VT
Siblings: One sister, younger; two brothers, one younger and one older
College: Lyndon State College
Degree: Psychology and Human Services
Married: No, one kid
Job: Public safety dispatcher and Vermont 911 officer

Crystal Lampman is a member of a large, well-known family in Swanton. When we meet in her home there, she tells me that her grandfather Blackie Lampman was the Abenaki chief when she was a girl. Crystal credits him, a native American with a sixth-grade education, for getting her to college; she was his first grandchild to bring home a college degree. Adopting her grandfather's credo of helping people, she interned in college at the St. Johnsbury Correctional Facility, providing career counseling for a young Abenaki "who was in the wrong place at the wrong time," as she put it. "He got caught up in some bad behaviors." After graduating she worked for Caring Communities as a Youth Outreach coordinator in Franklin County, briefly tried nursing, and joined the St. Albans Police Department in 2005 as a 911 dispatcher.

What's a typical day for a 911 dispatcher?

I take between five and ten calls on a typical day. There are two of us on at any given time. There can be upwards of four, depending on what's going on. We're answering for Franklin County; we're backup for the rest of the state of Vermont; and we're also the primary dispatchers for thirty-seven agencies in Franklin and Grand Isle Counties. We steer people to assistance. If necessary, we'll send the police, fire, rescue people. We'll remain on the line with the caller, letting them know we're there for them. Sometimes it just means small talk until the ambulance gets there. Keeping people calm, offering medical directives for them if they need it.

Does your nursing training come in handy on the job?

Absolutely.

Can you tell me a little about your involvement with the Abenaki community around Swanton?

When my grandfather was alive, my family was very, very involved.

He was Chief Leonard Lampman. I was very proud of him. He was a wonderful grandpa. I always thought it was great to go to his office . . . to see his headdress. In the early 1980s his main focus was educating the youth of the tribe. He was very involved in getting kindergarten to be part of the public school program. I went to private kindergarten. My younger brother was one of the first kids that went to public kindergarten. My grandfather did wonderful things in terms of helping native American students go to college. Abenakis, unfortunately, have a very low rate of young people continuing their education. That was something he really pushed to change.

Were there Abenaki ceremonial events when you were a kid?

Not, not so much. I can remember being part of the dance troop . . . I can remember going to like fishing derbies with my grandfather and my dad. I went to some pow-wows. Heritage Day [an annual celebration, with dancing, prayers, leadership meetings, and entertainment] didn't start until after my grandfather passed away when I was eight.

Did you feel any discrimination because you were Abenaki?

I never felt it. My dad and his siblings definitely were discriminated against. For my dad in high school it was mostly badmouthing. He wasn't part of the in-crowd. He got teased. He was one of eleven kids and they lived in . . . they lived in an old, ramshackle house and didn't have in-door plumbing.

Who makes up your community in Swanton? Work associates, family, friends?

It's some of each. My family's pretty involved in the community. My cousin is the chief of police. My uncle is president of the rescue squad; at one point the majority of the people on the squad were family. You know, I come from a huge family. Not only was my dad one of eleven kids, but there are thirty-five grandkids. So we've kind of hit all aspects of the community: in jobs, in the schools.

Without my family I wouldn't be able to take care of my daughter. I've got cousins and nieces that babysit for me. I've got a second cousin that my daughter calls grandma; it's another set of grandparents for her. We're one hundred percent involved in each other's lives. Nothing happens without someone in the family knowing about it.

My sister has four kids. My younger brother has three. Most of my cousins have two or three. Having eleven kids like my grandmother—I can't imagine it. (She laughs.) My grandmother amazes me. I don't know how she did it.

Some folks say we're in a dark economic era. What are your feelings on that?

I absolutely feel that we are; we're in a very difficult time right now. My dad has been without a job going on two years. He's an older worker, so it's been hard for him to find anything. Buying my own home this year has made me realize how expensive it is for day-to-day living: fuel, electricity, maintenance. I think it would be very difficult for young people just starting out to get a first mortgage. It was difficult; it took me about a year.

Are you optimistic about things getting better?

I'd like to be optimistic. It's hard because I see programs being cut where I know there's a need. Every day I see officers struggling to do their jobs, yet we're cutting human services programs that would, you know, take out a lot of the day-to-day struggles that people are having that are causing officers to have to intervene. I'd like to be optimistic, but sometimes it seems we are stuck in a tunnel.

What would you like to see help the economy in Vermont?

More jobs, better paying jobs. Jobs with benefits—that's huge. I loved working with Caring Communities when I was fresh out of college. It was my ideal job. I loved working with kids, I loved being in the schools. But, you know, it was great when it was just me. Then I had my daughter and there were no benefits—no health insurance at all. I had to leave the job that I loved to find a job that offered the things I needed for her.

How do you see jobs coming here to Franklin County?

(Crystal smiles painfully.) I hate to say it, but I don't think that things that people are fighting against are a bad idea. The fight over the Wal-Mart Store in St. Albans comes to mind. I remember wanting to protect Vermont, keeping the natural beauty. But at the same time I see the need for jobs coming in. They might not be great paying jobs, but they're jobs nevertheless. And they're jobs that are going to help somebody. If you got someone who's already on the system and is receiving Medicaid and food stamps and child care, by giving them a job you're giving them some hope. Sure, maybe they'll still remain on Medicaid and food stamps, but they're, you know, trying to contribute to society in some way, shape, or form.

What can we do to help people buy a piece of land, a house?

For one thing, the taxes are extreme. I own less than a quarter of an acre. My taxes are thirty-six hundred dollars a year. It's insane. I have the most respect for teachers, but when I see teachers threatening to walk a picket line because they want a raise and are being denied that raise—not everybody that's paying taxes that are paying their salaries is getting a raise. So they have to be reasonable. I mean, they have loans and bills they have to pay off, but so does Joe Schmo down the street who's not getting paid that salary and having the entire summer off.

Would you describe yourself as more intellectual, physical, or emotional?

I'm emotional. I do things because they make me feel good. It makes me feel good to help out my community and get something back. I couldn't imagine living anywhere else but Swanton. It's a wonderful, caring community.

My family just experienced two back-to-back deaths. And the community has just been amazing. My Aunt Joan who worked for rescue for thirty-plus years died of cancer. Her funeral procession was long and complicated; it had ambulances and fire engines from all over Franklin County. The Border Patrol did a fly by with a helicopter. Then Joan's daughter passed away less than a month after that from some heart complications. Again the community reached out to the whole family. That's just the way it's always been; whenever someone has needed something or experienced illness or death, the community comes together to support them.

Swanton has had a large number of men and women going to the wars in Iraq and Afghanistan. How has that hit you?

The call up of soldiers has been *so* difficult. My cousin is on his second tour. His first tour was in Iraq; his second tour is going to be in Afghanistan. He's twenty-nine. It's difficult to, you know, to readjust to life, coming back from this. It's scary. One of our parks patrol officers is nineteen years old, and he's headed for his first tour. It's scary to think of what he's going to see and face every day. We know he's not going to come back the same kid . . . and he's a great kid. It's going to be difficult for him to readjust.

Swanton has a huge number being called up. There are so many families affected in the local schools. Moms and dads are going. I wish that didn't have to happen. You know, I've seen friends sign up simply for the bonus. There's health care and benefits. Something happens, they know their family will be taken care of. But that's a scary thing to have to think of.

If you were to give me an executive summary of the last ten years of your life, what would you say you've accomplished? What have you done?

The biggest thing is making an impact and difference in my community. I've begun to raise a wonderful, intelligent little girl. I've become, you know, a stakeholder in Swanton by purchasing a home here; what happens matters to me now more than it did before. I want this to stay a great place to live. I want my daughter and her friends to be able to continue to think that this is a great place to live. So when they become adults, they choose to live here as well.

Getting my college degree was one of the biggest things for my family.

I'm going to ask you my classic Vermont questions: You ever milk a cow?

I've milked cows, growing up and helping out at friends' farms. Always by hand.

You ever tap maple trees?

I have. I have friends who own large operations in Fairfield and Bakersfield. I've collected buckets. My dad, up at Carmen Brook Farm in Highgate, has done traditional boiling. Every year they do a celebration. They take a birch bowl and pour the sap in and boil it, using hot rocks over an open fire. You drop rocks in the sap until it thickens. Then you dish them out and keep putting more hot rocks in. It's a celebration of springtime. They do tours. They have some caves that have hieroglyphics in them. You can go in and take a look.

Canning? You ever can food?

My mom was huge into canning. We'd do tomatoes, we'd do green beans, we'd do sweet pickles, sunshine pickles, Christmas pickles. We did corn. We made our own homemade salsa. I did the "girl chores," as my brothers would say. I had to help my mom get the canning together. I had to wash the jars . . . (smiles fleetingly at the memory) . . . yeah, I had to wash the jars . . . I had to help fill the jars. My mom would do the boiling process and tip the jars upside down. My little sister's job was to listen for the pop [signifying that the lid is properly sealed]. We had a dirt cellar in an old, dusty house. We kept potatoes there; we put them in bins. If the tomatoes were green and a frost was coming, we picked them and put them in bags and covered them with newspapers, to let them ripen. When I was growing up, my parents would alternate between having a cow slaughtered, then having a pig slaughtered, and filling the freezer up.

With four kids that was the easiest way to make it through the winter. My parents still do a big garden.

How about hunting and fishing?

Before college I went hunting with my dad often. I remember one year he sat me on the fence line because he didn't want me to get lost. He told me to stay by the trail I was at. My uncles and my cousins and my brothers were all in tree stands around me. If I got the first shot, and didn't get a clean shot, they could get another shot and take it down for me because my dad made me hunt with a .410 . . . a .410 single shot. (She laughs heartily.) That's all they would let me have was a .410 single shot.

Sitting on the fence, did you get cold?

Umm . . . nope, it wasn't too bad. I was well dressed. (Crystal continues right along with no prompting.) I've fished my entire life. Ice fishing. Summer fishing. I fished in the Missisquoi River. I've caught perch, I've caught sunfish. I've caught northern pike. I've caught catfish. We go bull-pout fishing in the spring from the river bank, where it's muddy; they like to go where it's muddy. When we were kids, my grandpa had a camp on Charcoal Creek, and we would fish from the back yard with throw-out lines and big bamboo poles. Now we just go down to the river bank here, which is kind of at the boat launch, by the bridge. And we fish. Or we go down to Louis's Landing and fish there.

How about winter sports?

For me, winters are to be inside, with something simmering on the stove and a good book. I love to read. I always have a couple of books going. I like mysteries. I read a lot of J.D. Robb, Patricia Cornwell. The forensic stuff, I like that. If my nieces are going to read it, I read it first. So I've read all the Twilight series books.

Are you interested in Vermont history?

Absolutely. I like to see how Vermont his changed from an agricultural state to industry. I had a lot of friends in farm families. Just watching how life has changed for them interests me. It's hard to have a small family farm now. You see the small farms grouping together to form corporations; that's kind of sad to me.

I think the crack that went down Vermont over civil unions was horrible. I don't think it had to happen the way it did. The Take Back

Vermont movement happened when I was in college. I was driving around and seeing the signs and being discouraged over that narrow-mindedness. *Are there still land ownership issues between Vermont and the Abenakis?* I believe most of that has been cleared up. The big thing was the burial ground on Monument Road. If we wanted to seek federal recognition now, it would be more for education purposes and health care benefits for some of the elderly folks. You know, the whole idea of casinos and a reservation is just kind of preposterous to us; it's not something we believe in. That's not something that we need here. It's great to be able to not really brag but just be proud of our heritage. It doesn't need to be stuck under other people's noses, and, "Ha, ha, look what we've got."

How about the future? What would like to see happen in the next ten years? What are you worried about?

(Takes a long pause.) I'm worried that Vermont won't be the kind of place my daughter can come back to and find a good job that will allow her to live here. I'm worried we'll continue to lose manufacturing jobs that are here. The closing of Vermont Yankee [now called Entergy Vermont] is going to have a huge impact on jobs in southern Vermont; it's going to push people out. I'm worried that the industry that's here won't be sustainable for long. I'm worried about the impact of war on this community. I've got nephews so I hope that by the time they're old enough, this is not still something we're still fighting. I have mixed feelings about us being in Afghanistan. The intellectual part of me understands why we need to be there, the emotional part wishes that we weren't there. We're dumping a lot of money into an area where we don't know what the impact will be, and there are people in our own country that are hurting. We're diverting the money away . . . a lot of money. We don't know how it's going to end. Maybe we set up this great infrastructure for them, and they turn on us. We won't have the ally we think we're going to have. I have a friend who just came back from his third tour, and he works with me in the police department in St. Albans. He showed me pictures of the roadside bombing he was involved in. It was an amazing thing he even came back to us; the part of me that knows that wishes we weren't there.

Do you use social media much?

I'm addicted to Facebook. I log in every night to stay caught up. It's the easiest way, the best way, to stay caught up with my friends from college. I spend an hour reading through the postings; it's much easier to do that than calling everybody on the phone. There are times I work until eleven o'clock at night; when I get home I'm not going to call any of them. Lots of my friends are Facebookers. Probably half the rescue squad is on Facebook. We tease each other about it; that's kind of funny. A lot of teachers are on Facebook, so we pass messages back and forth about how the kids are doing.

Final question: Do you have a favorite quote?

I do: "Shoot for the moon. Even if you miss, you'll still land among the stars." ∎

Fifteen, I was out on the street and still maintaining

Davon Martin

Born: August 25, 1985
Where: Concord, NC
Siblings: Three brothers, older; one sister, deceased
College: Dean College, Champlain College
Degree: Communications and Sociology from Dean College
Married: No
Job: Construction worker

> Black, six foot four, two hundred and fifty pounds, Davon Martin is not your typical young Vermonter. He wasn't born here and may not remain here, because of racial profiling and limited opportunities. Yet he loves the place, he tells me, when we talk in a brick house in the city's Old North End, a house in which Davon lived a good portion of the last decade after the family who owns the house took him in back in 2000.

When did you first come to Vermont?

I moved to Vermont in 1996, after living in Ohio for a while.

What brought you here?

My mom wanted my three older brothers to see their dying father (Davon's father was living in Arizona.) My mom wanted my three older brothers to have some time with their father.

So you're the youngest of four kids?

Five.

And you're the youngest?

I'm the youngest, I'm the baby.

All boys?

I had a sister, and she passed when she was thirteen.

Do you see your brothers much?

Yeah, I see my brothers. Any time they out of jail, I see them a lot.

Are they out of jail quite a bit?

It depends on the year, I have to say . . . it's like the seasons. You might have them here for summer, spring, but they might be gone for fall and winter.

Do they live here?

Yeah. All my three brothers live here. Two of them are out now, so I see them fairly a lot. [Davon makes it clear that the in-and-out-of-jail pattern was a staple of his family's life, not his personal life.] When I was fifteen my mom was selling heroin and she got busted. My mom and brothers were all going to jail. Everybody in my family was locked up. I was out on the street and stuff, but I was still maintaining and going to school. A classmate brought me home to this house to meet her parents. Me, her, her mom and dad, we sat down and talked. Next thing I knew, I was living here.

Looking at the last ten years in Vermont, if you were to summarize your experience, what would you say?

I'd have to say it was like a vacation that I learned a lot on. On my path to becoming an adult. It was a vacation from the sense of all the crime and drugs I had seen in Ohio, and stuff like that. It was more like a great escape, ironically. (He smiles.) We have a theme park [in Ohio] called the Great Escape.

Do you see a lot of drug business going on here now compared to ten years ago?

In general, in Burlington, you do. Like, right now, the problem is crack. And OxyContin. But Vermont is kind of known as a weed place. People smoke weed. That hasn't changed. As far as the introduction of over-the-counter drugs, and easier-access drugs, people are taking more pharmaceuticals to the next plateau. You see that a lot. During high school we saw it when it was truly hitting. A good five percent of the kids out of our graduating class, to this day, are addicted to o.c.'s and stuff. Our class [Burlington High School 2004] was like the beginning stages of it in high school. It was starting to grow, and now it's a big problem.

How did you get on the college track?

I really didn't know of college.

It wasn't part of your career track.

(Shakes his head no.) It wasn't something taught to me as a kid growing up . . . going to college. You play sports or you sell drugs to make it out of the hood, per se. My friend's parents worked college into my head, and I went right after graduation, into college. I went to a junior college in Franklin, Mass, Dean College, to kind of get my feet underneath me. I studied communications and sociology.

I liked going to school there. But it was tough because I quit playing football and people got mad at me because the football team wanted me to keep on playing. So I became enemies against the football team once I quit.

What position did you play?

I played both sides of the ball. Tight end and defensive tackle. I stopped playing because of the politics of seniority—he'd been here, so the person should start o ver you. But in my eyes the best talent should be on the field because you're here to win. At the same time I didn't feel like giving it my all anymore because in college I seen better opportunities than just playing football to make a living. I wanted to have a body, be able to walk. And look at me now, I'm walking instead of saying (a soft, pained groan) "I played football . . . I can't move my back." Yeah, I got done with hurtin', bangin' up people. I like having a body. Basketball's more my sport these days. It's physical, but I don't have to hit you at full speed.

Then you returned to Burlington and went to Champlain College?

I did two years [at Champlain College], but things didn't work out because I had my mom get diagnosed with cancer and me not focusing because of all these family issues—brothers going to jail and stuff like that. Now I have a year left to finish. I'm in no rush to go back and be back in debt. (Davon says that he's now framing rooms, sanding floors, banging nails.) All the stuff I'm learning, when I own my own house some day, I won't have to pay somebody to come do stuff that I already know how to do.

In your personal history in Vermont the last decade, what were your high and low points?

The high point, my best memory, was senior year in high school. I can't lie. I did stuff that most high school seniors don't get to do. I made it to two state championships, in basketball and football. Even though I lost both, I was grateful to have the opportunity because I know a lot of high school kids who wish they had that opportunity. The basketball finals were in Patrick [Gymnasium in Burlington]. It's fun to play there. You get the UVM atmosphere. You feel like you're playing on the biggest stage Vermont has to offer.

My low point was my mom and brothers all going to jail. Everybody in my family was locked up when I was fifteen years old. So that was one of my lowest points ever. And my mom having cancer. I don't know . . . I think they were about equal low points. You felt kind of an abandonment. But you know . . . the grace . . . I found my friend's parents who took me in. So I got another opportunity, another view of life I didn't have before. I'm grateful for that.

Do you know much about state history?

No, I really don't know much. I know some things by word of mouth.

Like I know the basics of Ethan Allen and the Green Mountain Boys. I know that on North Street there's a pole put intentionally in the ground for war veterans. It's where they found remains of soldiers, but now they covered it so people can't tamper with it. It's kind of cool. It's my most in-depth look at local history. I saw it when I started jogging. I jogged by there.

Vermont and America have been having rough economic times. Do you feel that we're entering a kind of dark era or dark age?

I'm kind of fifty-fifty. I feel that every superpower throughout history has declined. And it seems like America's time to decline. But at the same time, I have the idea of American spirit to rebuild and take the country to a different approach. I hope America is not just seen as this working place of blonde hair, blue-eyed people, and more like America the land of the free. The whole idea of the melting pot—I would like to see that be more presented in the worldwide view of how people see America. And I think that will happen because you've got generations like mine, which are really diverse, compared to the old generations ahead of us.

Do you think opportunities will be good for you in Vermont?

For me, personally, not really. I think it's like a twenty-five percent chance for me to like find a career in Vermont and really hone my skills at it. Because it seems like you need to leave Vermont, get a career, save money, and then move back. It's kind of like you got to wait for the jobs to be created in Burlington for you to have your chance. You've got to leave and come back and check in to see if you can get that job to come back. Cause I'd love to live in Vermont. It's more of a relaxing place and the place I'd want to raise my kids, if I ever have them.

Like Richmond. It's close enough to Burlington but it's far enough so I can still have peace and quiet. There's more of a wilderness feel to it. They got the gorge and everything, swimming.

If you leave the state, where would you go?

Out west. Houston. A bunch of opportunities in Texas. Ain't just big for steak. Got opportunities. Lot of people make money out there.

Do you consider yourself a physical, intellectual or emotional person?

That's a good question. I see myself as all three. But hmm . . . I'd say I'm more mental because I'm analytical. I analyze things before I give my final input. My own saying I came up with is, Before you have an open heart,

you have to have open ears. So you need the open ears and the open heart to take you further on.

Where did you get this open attitude towards the world?

I have to say that the way I started to look at the world this way was reading Langston Hughes. I read a lot of Langston Hughes. He's like my favorite poet. People don't realize he wrote plays. I'm into a lot of black history stuff. History, in general, to see where we come from and see how I can make myself a better person.

Do you know much about Vermont geography?

I went on my own discovery after I graduated from high school. I found Lake Seymour. (Davon laughs, happy with the memory.) That summer, to find adventure, we just got in the car to find a town. It's cool how sometimes I feel more accepted in the rural places than I do in Burlington. It's a weird, complex thing. Sometimes I'll walk in these diners and get something to eat with Tak, a Vietnamese guy. And they'll be, "Well, how you doing?" It's like they're welcoming as opposed to in Burlington where they look at you like, "Oh my God, how are these two guys friends?" And they got to be hostile. So, yeah, I think me and my friends have taken it upon ourselves to kind of learn the small town idea of Vermont. It means something to people who live in this state, and I think I came across that.

Do you go to church? Are you a religious guy?

I was until my mom gave me the choice. Once I turned twelve, she gave me the choice to keep on doing Jehovah's Witness or the Baptist Church. I kind of became more of an agnostic. I understood there is some spiritual being in the world who created us all, but at the same time I don't believe in how people have used a God creature-being to say the world is this, this, and this. People use religion to gain power and control over people. Now I'm more like . . . whatever. I like the ideas of all religions and make my own. (He smiles.) Back in the day I used to sing in the choir.

How about your peers? How do you get along with them in Vermont?

Some Vermont kids are very hesitant to do new things. And a lot of people fear the six-four, two-fifty, big black guy my age. And there's a lot of people open minded. I grew up with a bunch of really diverse people, social-wise and culturally. I'm still friends today with kids whose parents are multi-millionaires and with others who are lower class, just like me. So I have to say to my peers, Once you allow people to have an open ear and an open heart, I think anybody will welcome you in.

As a big black guy, do you get racially profiled?

Oh yeah. The first thing I have to say about my years living in Vermont is how many times the cops stopped me and said I fit a description because I was a tall, black kid. The first time it ever happened is when the cop didn't see that I had my headphones on, and he pulled out his gun on me because I didn't stop. That was the worst time ever. He should have known, at least, that I had a PeeWee football helmet and shoulder pads and pants, all in my other hand. I don't see the need to pull out a gun on a twelve-year-old kid.

Anybody that can evoke the fear in people gets profiled. I guess it depends on the person's size, how they carry themselves, the way they present: I definitely would say Burlington still has a racial problem, but people are hidden about it. The problem is nobody wants to talk about the issue in Burlington because nobody wants to offend nobody. But you are offending everybody because you want to talk about it in your house, in your comfort zone. You should get out and talk to more people about it, you know.

How about Hispanics in Burlington, do they have confrontations with the law?

It's gotten better. At the same time you have a bunch of old school, traditional people who do not open their eyes to accept everybody. How can I say it? (Davon adopts an innocent, cringing voice.) "We accept everybody, I go to church, and I'm such a good person." (He drops the pantomime.) But then, when you see me walking on the street, you grab all your personal belongings tighter, and you clinch 'em. (He adopts a third tone of voice.) It's like, "I worked late, sir. I don't need to steal your pocket book or anything." (He shakes his head and stares at me.) I don't see why people fear me at all.

What are your personal feelings about white people? Did you ever have a black Panther attitude back in the day?

Yeah, I definitely did have that kind of attitude. It started when I was real little, when *Malcolm X* came out. My mom made sure I watched that movie. Every black kid went. If it was on TV, my mom made sure I watched *Malcolm X*. So I got into it. My mom grew up in New York, in the Bronx, and she was accepted as white. So, you know, she kind of understood both sides of the equation. She made sure I knew black history. In the South, too, because I was called a nigger, and my first days were bad going to school, I had some prejudice. But at the end of the day, my mom always taught me to be open and to never let my ignorance ever shadow the way I invited people in. My mom was very good at making sure I was accepting of people. Treat people the way you want to be treated. That's the thing she installed in my head.

Who do you trust?

Mostly now I put my trust in friends, family, myself. If you come into my life, you will earn trust. It's not just I trust you right off the bat—how many people are like that in this world? It's like anything; you earn trust when you have relationships.

And you have a girlfriend. Or are you married?

Oh no, no, no. (Waves both hands.) She has her own apartment, and I have my own. But we stay at each other's places for, like, weeks on end. It works out. It keeps things spicy.

You had the power to change something in Vermont, what would it be?

I'd like to see more diversity—not just cultural and ethnic diversity; I'd like to see social-class diversity the most. It seems in Burlington the small person is not heard that much. It seems like people up on the hill makes all the rules and the decisions. Even though it is starting to get different because this side of town [the Old North End] is cheaper, and a lot of middle-class people are moving to this side of town. So you're getting a little more influence, but not from the lower class.

I'd like to see police officers get more aware of their own personal attitudes. I think every police officer should have to do a racial-profiling class every two to five years—not just one to become a police. If there's somebody doing crime, get them. Don't just constantly profile people. Too many times—last summer, for instance—the police officers took pictures of us. Every time we're out there, at 4:30, on the basketball court. Fifteen minutes later a police officer is right there, watching us play basketball for the three hours we there in the summer. What for? Is it because black people congregate at Pomeroy Park in the summer? Is it that thing of evoking the fear in people that something is going to go on? Man . . . .

And this is black guys pickup basketball?

Yeah. Everybody's there. The only time we see like a dominant congregation of black folk in Burlington is at that basketball court. And it's kind of funny, cause when the talent was up there, at one point we got rated in *Sports Illustrated* as 72nd in the nation as talent at a local park. We got

Vermont noticed a little bit, playing basketball there. In America, ranked 72nd as talent at the park, that means something to me. It's kind of cool.

My classic Vermont questions: You ever milk a cow?

No.

Ever tap a maple tree?

No. But I'd love to.

Have you ever canned food?

Yeah, yeah, I did that before; that's nothing new to me.

You like getting your hands in the dirt?

I do. That should be a requirement of high school. Do something that relates to the state, like gardening and composting.

What's your cultural scene? You read, listen to music?

(He reminds me that he reads poetry, plays.) Music is big in my life. I grew up, my mom having me listen to seventies soul. The planet Lovetron . . . that whole idea. Then I got my own thing. I like Rick James. Prince. That Rick James and Prince era of music. I like rap. Jazz is more like the music I really wanted to understand because it has so many sounds in it. It shows pain and sorrow and happiness. It just has every emotion tied into it. Miles Davis, Satch-mo, I could keep on going.

Do you have a favorite quote?

(Later, Davon sends me an email with two poems by Langston Hughes:)

Justice
That Justice is a blind goddess
Is a thing to which we black are wise:
Her bandage hides two festering sores
That once perhaps were eyes.

The White Ones
I do not hate you,
For your faces are beautiful, too.
I do not hate you,
Your faces are whirling lights of loveliness and splendor, too.
Yet why do you torture me,
O, white strong ones,
Why do you torture me? ∎

I have no plans to get old

Nathan Merrill

Born: Middlebury, VT
When: February 22, 1978
Siblings: One sister, younger
Degree: None
Married: No
Job: Mechanic

Nathan Merrill is a wiry and restless young man. Twice his movements knock my recorder off the arm of the sofa, dropping it to the floor, deleting big chunks of digital data. Not that I should be surprised. "I usually don't talk to strangers," he told me not long after we sat down in the spare room of a friend's house in Burlington, then glanced at my photographer and added, "I'm feeling a little cramped in this room with the two of you." Slowly, he does warm a little to my questioning and soon reveals an inner patriotic fervor attested to by frequent references to history, usually the history of war. He also informs me that for a blue-collar mechanic he has an IQ of 142 and left home at seventeen with twenty dollars in his pocket and never looked back. "Everything I have," he says. "I made."

But you were raised in Ripton, Vermont, right?

I am a child of the mountain in Ripton back when it was, indeed, a small town.

Is that where your parents were from?

(Shakes his head no, long hair shifting on his shoulders.) My father grew up in Middlebury. My mother's an Army brat. She was born at Ford Ord, Monterrey, California. She grew up in Munich. In fact, she remembers being there when [President] Kennedy was shot. Her high school years were Lisbon Falls, Maine, of all places, while my maternal grandfather was serving fifty months in the glorious Republic of South Vietnam. But as I said, I have no family at all. We have not spoken in at least a decade.

Is that something I can ask you more about or should I leave it alone?

You can roll as you wish, doctor.

(A pause on my part.) Okay, why don't you tell me about your job?

I'm a mechanic. I would be insulted if anybody ever called me an automotive technician. Technicians just change parts. Mechanics actually know how it works and will attempt to fix it, if necessary.

How'd you learn the trade?

I had a mentor. A guy named Amos Langdon Roleau III. Owned a business called Packard of Vermont. Out in New Haven. He owned a shop and a junk yard, but he didn't really want it anymore. So he'd stop in the shop and if I was stuck on something he'd share the benefit of his experience with me. For the most part I learned my trade the hard way. I worked solo.

At Packard of Vermont I worked mostly on old, vintage cars. And Volvos; they're my specialty. Many garages now don't do serious repair. Too messy. I don't want to work in a cream-puff shop where you don't have the option of getting used parts for your customers. (Shifts around, stretching his legs, spreading both arms.) You know, the EPA is trying to shut down every junk yard they can. So when somebody dies, and their heir wants to run that thing, it's not impossible but difficult. It's like you have to realize, unless people are going to stop owning complex machines and driving cars, we've got to have some designated areas for the broken and the bleeding and make a mess. At a lot of shops it's a different world. Everything is new. The repair bills are huge. The hourly rates in Chittenden County are exorbitant.

When did you first get interested in cars?

(Cocks his head and smiles.) Since I first had Legos. But what I really like are planes. (A born storyteller, he waits a while and then says) I bought one for my birthday. My twenty-ninth. It's a Pietenpol Air Camper [a simple, home-built plane]. A Polish immigrant to the United States designed it. The first of them appeared in 1929. Mine is the Continental model. She's a lady in waiting . . . in a shipping container . . . still looking for an engine. She's at my friend's farm; I just parked her behind the horse barn . . . the whole container.

Do you spend much time in the air?

A number of people call me when they need somebody to hold down the other side of the airplane or deliver an airplane somewhere. I'm flattered to have acquaintances who ask me to move airplanes around for them, even with the knowledge that I have not yet finished my private pilot's license. I don't have that little piece of paper. There's places where you just never, never get caught. In Alaska, the majority of people who fly, if a survey was taken, would be found not to have a license. It's not a widely-discussed thing in the aviation community.

If you like planes, how come you're fixing cars instead of flying or fixing planes?

By many means do we gain the experience to pursue our ultimate goals. I needed a junk-yard education in how things work, but even more importantly in how things break. I want to work on airplanes, but that in itself is also a pit stop. I want to build them. I want to design and build something that people like me can afford to fly, something that's fun, and you should be able to get into the air for twenty-five or thirty grand. Build it, which you would have to . . . and (he fairly gushes) have fun!

I found something beautiful on the Internet the other day, speaking of aircraft. It's called the Radial Rocket. Made out of the Danaev M14P Radial. Three hundred and sixty horsepower. It resembles aesthetically nothing so much as a Grumman F-8 Bearcat . . . a piston-engine Navy fighter that missed the war [World War II]. It's currently the fastest piston-engine aircraft in the entire world. There's one with clipped wings running on alcohol out of Reno called Rare Bear.

You really are into airplanes.

(Nathan veers off on a story.) I was with my whole family. I'll never forget it in my entire life. My mother walked us all around the Mall until my right foot was swollen up and wouldn't bend any more. Then we were going to the Air and Space Museum, which, of course, I had lived and breathed and gone on this whole trip [to Washington, DC] to see. So, we're looking at the P-40 in the lobby. But there's a big, tall, A-frame ladder setting next to the Spirit of St. Louis hanging from the ceiling. And there's an old man sitting in the Spirit of St. Louis. I asked a minor staff member— happened to be a custodian mopping the floor; I figured these people know everything that goes on in this place. I asked, "What are they doing, inspections on the air frame, making sure it's not going to rot and fall off the ceiling?" The guy looked at me and chuckled and said, and these are his exact words, "Shit, kid, that's Jimmy Doolittle." Up in the plane! (He shoots an arm toward the ceiling.) Sitting in it . . . just sitting there. My eleven-year-old butt stood at the bottom of the ladder for the next forty-five minutes until General Doolittle felt like coming down. And I shook hands with . . . I don't know what else to say: with a Jedi master.

These days do you have any big plans for working on airplanes?

(A long, lung-emptying sigh.) I would like my name to be known by the time I check out of this world. But I hesitate to say such an egotistical thing.

Okay, let's shift to the economy. Some folks think that America's in a dark economic era. What do you think?

We're paying for our greed and gluttony. Those who accumulate huge, unneeded homes, material goods, live with a white elephant.

But I live in the sticks. There you notice it affects people differently. They're driving junk because it's paid for. People are not spending money. People are worried. You can see how people are worried about money in how they take care of their cars, whether they buy tires or stretch what they got. I know folks who are shooting food; what they're not raising they're shooting. To me, that's beautiful. Self-sustainability. Independence. True independence is something people have to work for and sacrifice to have.

Have you ever worked much on big farm equipment?

Yeah. Farm equipment's easy. Big, gummy, simple stuff. You don't even need a tool stand. You need big wrenches and a serious air compressor and an inch-drive impact tool.

You can't buy a good farm tractor any more, did you know that? They're trash! Anything under two hundred horsepower is junk. They try to make too much power with too little engine, and the tractor doesn't weigh enough to be the brutal, blunt instrument that a farm tractor is. It's crazy, but all my friends who own farms are going back to seventies and eighties Internationals and Olivers. Yeah, they got two or three thousand pounds of cast iron in them, or more.

Are these small farmers? Are there many small farmers in Addison County?

A lot of them are play farmin'. It's a tax write-off for them. When I drive down the road, and I see it, I snicker. You can't compare one person's operation to their neighbor's; they're all different, but some of them small farmers just do it because it's cool—you know what I mean? It's the hip thing to do. Other people are trying to make a living by it. One clue to which one of those is which is what they drive. A real farmer drives something paid for, except maybe the big operations are always trading up their pick-ups; the old man's always got a new pick-up and they pass the others down the line.

Do you follow Vermont politics at all?

Only to the point that I'm appalled by what it's become. I think all politicians are liars. The liberals try to fix everything and Vermont has a habit of jumping on bandwagons. Too fast a response to a crisis is a weakness, not a strength.

I think there ought to be a law passed that you have to have at least raised children [here] or lived here for a certain amount of time before you're allowed to be a lawmaker. That gets back to the fact that us natives are losing our way of life. And we are. It's being frickin' legislated out from under us, at state and local levels.

What would you like to see happen to change that? What would you like to see in the future?

I'd like to get my work situation straightened out . . . but I have no plans to get old. I'll check out about the time my body starts to quit and I'm not useful anymore. You can't really put a number on it.

Then how about the past? Are you interested in Vermont history?

Oh yeah. I'm fascinated with Ira Allen. Most history focuses on his drunken, redneck brother Ethan. Ira Allen was the Thomas Jefferson of Vermont. He was the fella who essentially drafted the constitution of the republic of the Green Mountains. That's my understanding; I haven't had the time to research it adequately. I've been thinking of taking a Saturday morning and going to the Middlebury College library and giving myself a headache getting informed.

Some people might find me a bit separatist, but I love my home. That's Vermont. And I am interested in local history. Primarily where the old mills were, where the old towns were. I like to go digging the old sites of towns that were moved. Brandon is a good example, although the site has been well dug. The archaeology of the French and Indian War fortifications is really neat. And I like running the old roads around Bristol. Their purpose was to facilitate the movement of troops, artillery, and supplies north and south by means other than—this was like in 1797 or 1798—other than Lake Champlain. If we were going to face off against the British Royal Navy again, we needed to be able to move men and supplies, and especially artillery, north and south. And to this day, trying to get east and west in Vermont sucks. But there's a great north-to-south network, and it began back then.

Who makes up your community?

My dog. (He sort of laughs.) Trust is a very precious thing. You might call me careful.

Do you consider yourself more of an emotional, intellectual, or physical guy?

I do have a layman's streak of the intellectual in me. I'm empathic. I'm an antenna (he grins), so I work with cars. I'm actually what's known as an intuitive diagnostician. It gives me at least equal results as formal training. That's where my junkyard background—how things break—comes in. Ever look at a car and just see what ails it when it's setting and running in front of ya? You just close your eyes, and look towards the car with your eyes closed—I'm not joking with you—and in your brain ends up a statement somewhere along the lines of, Well, I can't prove it, but I think this. (Stretches his arms wide, twists one behind his head). I'm not like some dealer technician who says, "This component is broken." In the junkyard I've seen a car smashed in an accident. I know what's inside it; I know how it works and have gained some insight over time and with experience and

repetition. That means I know how it fails too, which means I can think my way around the problem.

Back to this idea of being empathic and an antenna. Do you have any kind of karmic sensibility for history or the future?

I am completely aware how I died in two previous lifetimes. But I don't talk about these things that much. You should know that just in case you see me start to squirm a little bit over here. It's not something I speak of openly. But, at the time, you asked me a difficult question that is not easy for me to answer with truth. (And he stops talking.)

I'm interested in the arc of each person's life, how they got to where they are and some sense of where they want to go. What is interesting in your talking about prior lives—

(Interrupting me) I'm an unreconstructed soldier. I am actually living this lifetime, and it feels like I'm just waiting for a moment which may or may not come. But which I, among the few people I know, am prepared for. I don't know how to say this, but it is one of my life's regrets that I have not tested myself in combat. Not the kind of button-pushing, screen-watching warfare that's generally conducted these days, but person-to-person.

Then why did you choose not to go into the military?

Got a dog to take care of.

A lot of troops we send overseas now are in their forties, and even their fifties.

Thirty-two is the cut-off for enlistment age . . . unless I wanted to be in the Guard. If I wanted to do something, I'd join the Marine Corps and work as hard as I could to become a long-range reconnaissance sniper. That's what I'd do. But they'd probably make me a truck driver. They take somebody with a pre-existing pilot's license and instead of giving them military aircraft training make them cook.

You don't meditate, do you?

I shoot. Unless you've done it seriously, it's hard to explain how truly meditative shooting is. I'll try to give you an insight.

There are six steps to firing a shot. The first one is sight alignment: the relationship between front and rear sights. The second one is sight picture: what the picture you made with your sight alignment looks like. [The third is] respiratory pause; your breath moves your body; your body can't move, which means that you're gonna take the shot at a consistent point in your breathing cycle—it's usually at the end of your exhale. Depending on your cardio-vascular condition, you have anywhere between two and eight seconds, before you breathe again. Step four is complicated: keeping your mind focused on your front sight. There are three ocular points: your rear sight, your front sight, and your target. The human eye can only focus on one point at a time. Focus on keeping that front sight on your target. Step five is, Squeeze the trigger, and there are twelve *e*'s in squeeze. Take your time . . . you don't snatch it, pull it, grab it because your hand going like this (moves his hand slightly) will move the rifle. Then follow through. Follow through is two things: it's physical and it's mental. Your mental follow through is you're going to absolutely freeze; you're not going to flinch, you're not going to do anything until you think the words "follow through" in your head. You will not release the trigger until after having thought those words in your head. The physical part is you will take a mental snapshot of what your sight picture looked like when the shot went off. A good rifleman who pays attention and follows through will know where every shot went, whether it was good or bad. Therefore, a rifleman never wastes a shot. Even the bad ones teach you something. In order to do this, you have to put yourself in what is referred to as your shooters bubble. There's nothing in your bubble; there's no hot, no cold, no rain, no bug, no nothing . . . only your sights and your target.

If you were to sum up the last ten years of your life, the first decade of the new millennium, what would you say?

I have survived.

Okay, I'm going to ask you my classic Vermont questions: You ever milk a cow?

Ayup.

You ever do any canning?

Oh my God, we had this four-acre garden when I was growing up. We canned anything: brussel sprouts, beets, carrots, whatever grew. We pickled eggs. Stored things in the basement. I never want to do it again.

You hunt or fish?

I don't have time to hunt anymore. I was a fair-to-middlin' hunter. I grew up with a Springer [spaniel] and a cut-off Savage [shotgun]—still have it. I liked the early fall bird season before deer hunting in November. October is my favorite time of year. It's not too hot, no bugs. There's just something about that fall air that makes me feel like a primitive savage hunting for my food. A very, very intense feeling. I'm a pretty down-to-earth guy when it comes to that stuff. It's also the saddest time of the year for me (and his voice suddenly plummets a couple octaves). Watchin' all the leaves die, and everythin'—I don't like winter very much. I hibernate. Too skinny for that shit.

What do you do to get through the winter?

Build model airplanes. Work on my guns. Shoot. I read a lot—keeps the brain busy and puts the body to sleep. But I sleep very little.

What do you like to read?

I'm a prolific reader. I read everything . . . almost everything. What people consider to be contemporary literature, I find it utterly wasteful of my time. I get to the end of books of that genre, and I'm like, Why did I just read that? This author just went on for two hundred and some odd pages, and I don't know why at the end of it. What was the point?

Music? As long as it's not country. I did play the trumpet. My lips are out of shape.

You use social media at all?

Negative. I don't even own a computer.

Do you have a favorite quote?

I'm going to go with John Paul Jones standing in front of the Second Continental Congress: "It seems a law once inevitable and inexorable that he who will not risk cannot win." ∎

You got to have some gut instincts

Eamon O'Shea

Born: October 13, 1978
Where: Burlington, VT
Siblings: One brother, younger; one sister, younger
Married: Yes, one kid
Job: Innkeeper; bartender

> I meet Eamon O'Shea in his house, his wife having taken their nine-month old daughter shopping. He's going over a pile of receipts from his Sheady Acres project, five small, funky, rentable cabins that he's in the process of opening and is marketing via Craigslist and other venues. The pile is high, a result of the length and complexities of building a business to serve the public in rural Vermont. In an hour or so he has to drive down to Montgomery Center and tend bar for the night at a local hot spot where Wednesdays are busy because drinks and food are cheap. Eamon shifts the pile of receipts and we sit at his table, sunlight flowing in through the western windows.

We're in this dark economy, and you've jumped into this entrepreneurial venture. Given the economy, do you have worries that it might tank?

Not really. I'm not really too worried about it tanking. The economy's definitely not helping me. The mountain is a very good indicator. I work up there a couple days a week, and the numbers are way way down at Jay Peak, for everything. A year ago this past weekend, there were twice as many skiers there. The new hotel is not doing very well. Their "cheap, steep, and deep" motto has gone out the window.

Jay Peak—who knows what's going to happen up there in five years? They do have balls up there, I have to say that. They have big balls. (He mentions the big new hotel, water park, golf course, and intense real estate focus.) I perceive my business succeeding because it's unique in the area. It's providing something that's not available, a couple's type atmosphere. The people that stay with us, they're more into skiing half the time, then doing other stuff: snowshoeing, cross-country skiing, sightseeing. I got people who go up to Montreal for the day, who go across to Sutton to check that out. More of your adventurous types who aren't just going to hammer out eight hours on the mountain every day.

Opening Sheady Acres, what were the easiest and hardest things to deal with?

To tell you the honest-to-God's truth, there wasn't much easy about it. The question I get asked the most is, "If you'd known how difficult this was going to be, would you have still done it?" And the answer is, "Depends which day you ask me."

Just seeing how much work I have into the project is amazing, totally amazing. I guess I've been pretty guilty about being naive about how much work, and how much money we were going to have to put into this. I got completely schooled by the State of Vermont, by the sheer scale of the project taken on by a private contractor with no crew. But I'm really happy with the results so far. We've had nothing but good feedback.

You're a classic entrepreneur. You knew what you were going to have to do, you'd never have done it.

You'd never do it. My wife, Shawna, she's completely the opposite. She'll research things to death. She just won't do them. She'll just research and research and research.

I, basically, had this idea in one day. I went to the bank. As soon as the money was in place, I didn't think about it twice. I was sick of, you know, doing these menial jobs and not really getting anywhere. I miss traveling, I miss a few things, but it's pretty fulfilling to have a project that you're putting all your energy into. Of course, we didn't plan on having a baby and starting the project at exactly the same time. That's just the way it came down. On the morning we dug the first scoop of dirt, I was on my way out the door with my muck boots on and Shawna said, "Oh, I'm pregnant."

But the biggest hurdle, to be honest, was my lack of knowledge about the way things work. I had no idea what was an issue and what wasn't. Things I thought were going to be a big issue weren't; things I thought would be minor became the biggest hurdles. The state . . . I can completely understand why there are building codes. Why Act 250 [Vermont's environmental development law] exists. I get that. That's why this state looks the way it does. But things just get so bureaucratic at times. I had to send in probably five hundred pieces of paper to the state. It was a box of paperwork. Without my brother [Brendan O'Shea sits on the Act 250 Review Board], I'd have had to hire someone to do that, because it's written in a different language. It's written in lawyer speak and state speak.

Everyone wants a little chunk of change. I kept trying to get around being a commercial venture. But once you're letting the public in your door, you're commercial. And you know, everybody likes to sit back and watch you get beat up.

That's the nature of humanity.

Yeah. (Eamon chuckles.) If I could count the times a certain lawyer we know was rubbing his hands together and watching me get thrown to the wolves . . . people just love that, you know. But when all is said and done, people at the state level were very reasonable. You just have to get on their wavelength. It was not a wavelength I was on.

Now I've got three livable cabins, with nice beds, flat-screen TVs, everything you need. And a fourth one half way done. During the summer I was putting in over eighty hours a week. I was out there twelve to fourteen hours a day. Just every available minute of daylight. I think I'm going to finish the project at around two hundred and fifty thousand dollars, which isn't exorbitant for what it is. If we can rent each cabin one hundred days a year, I figure we'll be in pretty good shape.

Nobody can prepare you for what you're going to have to deal with, the human factors: calling, booking, canceling, people just not showing up. Most people have been very respectful, so far. They're kind of like we are: like to travel, like the funky side of things. The business kind of morphs itself. It will become what it will become, on its own, if you give it some direction. It's going to do what it does. People are going to make it.

What's your vision for the next five years?

I see a five-year-old daughter in kindergarten . . . I see us spending the winters and summers here, working hard. We've talked about another commercial venture on the property. A pub, a public house sort of thing. We really really miss traveling. We want to be able to get out of here for a few weeks, at least in the fall and the spring. Just take off, bring Quinn with us. It's hard to look into the future with this. Some days, you know, I just want to turn around and sell it and move back to Jackson and ski powder. Other days I remember why I'm not doing that right now.

It's also given me a lot of other avenues in the building trades. Last summer, I had no less than ten people ask me to build one for them. People ask me if they can cut them down and take them away.

They're on posts. Make me the right offer, I just might do it.

Your grandfather Bun O'Shea was a champion of the Democratic Party in the 1950s. He ran against Vermont legend Senator George Aiken, just to give him an opponent. Do many people know of the rich political history of the O'Sheas in Vermont?

No one under the age of forty. People generally, under forty, aren't that political, I find. But it depends. When I go places and there are older people, a lot of them know my grandfather, Bun O'Shea. I talk to my cousin, Casey, who works in the Capitol Building in Washington—he's the first grandson of Bun, and he's keeping it real down there. He deals with the top guns on a daily basis. So it's not totally over. As for the O'Sheas in Vermont, I don't know how many people know of us any more.

What are your feelings about politics in the state?

I'm interested in state politics. Town politics more so . . . I get into the town meeting and that stuff. I've lived in a lot of other towns [besides Montgomery] with a lot more rules. I'm all about less rules. I think people generally let you be here. You can be as involved or not involved as you want. Not to bring it back to the cabins, but people said the town was going to be my big hurdle. And they were great. I told them what I was doing. I don't think it hurts that I live here, I'm from here. I like the fact we have no law enforcement. You tell that to people from Massachusetts and they want to move here. I like the town politics, generally.

Are you a Vermont history buff?

I'm pretty knowledgeable about Vermont history. I read *Fast Lane*. I find it interesting that the state's been here so long that the history almost gets covered up a little bit. Vermont, as far as places go, doesn't have that much history. Stuff has happened here, but it's the history of a small place; it's not like anything insanely radical has happened. We're famous for gay marriage. It's like, Yeah, a lot worse things have happened.

Do you consider yourself more of a physical, emotional, or intellectual guy?

I try to keep it a pretty good balance. I'd like to be more physical. I miss the days when I would go and beat the shit out of myself on a mountain, and not have anything else to think about but work that night. I think it's good to be able to turn off the intellectual part. It's pretty hard not to be emotional when you have a baby in the house and get dragged into the mom and baby thing.

Speaking of the mom and baby thing, how has the project been for Shawna?

I think it's been better for her than she realizes. While we were doing the cabins and she was pregnant, it crossed my mind that it would be great for Shawna to be able to work out of the house and spend time with the baby, because who wants to have a baby and go back to work in two months, then drop the baby off with strangers every day? But she didn't go for the idea. She said, "I don't want to be scrubbing toilets." And who does? But I think that in the long run she's going to think it's a pretty good thing. All this got dropped on her head all at once. She has a bigger role than I expected. She deals with all the credit card stuff, the paperwork; she cleans the cottages. I think it's good for Quinn, too, being in this atmosphere. What kid wouldn't want to grow up with five tiny houses to play in?

What were you doing at the start of the decade, back on January 1, 2000?

I was in a riot in Whitefish, Montana. Thirty people got arrested. Flipped over a cop car. I was living in Whitefish, tuning skis. Living the Montana life. Probably the only boozier place than Vermont I've ever been. We were there in 2001 as well, came back here and built a tree house. We lived in a tree house for four years. Then moved out to Jackson. To tell you the truth, if I could afford to live there, if I could ever do something like this there, I'd probably still be there. But it beats you down; you can't live forever with roommates. Some people can. But I can't.

Over the last decade can you remember your high and low points?

Obviously, having a baby is a high point. There are times I'm extremely satisfied when I look outside and see what I've done with the property. The low points really came repeatedly at the end of the ski seasons, when you've done nothing but ski bum the entire year, and you look back and say, I had such a good time doing that . . . but really (he chuckles) what really did I accomplish?

My classic Vermont questions: You ever milk a cow?

More than one. I've done some milking in the Stebbins barn [in Enosburg]. I wouldn't want to make a career of it.

You ever tap maple trees?

Both in my yard, and in a legitimate sugarbush.

How about canning food? Ever put food by?

I haven't. We used to have a big garden before the business and the baby. But we never got into canning. It's a lot of work. I'd rather brew than can.

You still brewing?

I've gotten back into it. But the waste water thing with breweries is scary. That's why so many breweries have to brew off site. They brew in an industrial building, then they bring the beer into their pub instead of brewing it right there.

You hunt or fish?

I've never gone hunting. I used to fish a lot.

What are your concerns for the future of Vermont and for our region in particular?

I can't help but worry about the weather; I'm so dependent on it. Both global warming and your average Vermont weather, which is so much crazier than anywhere else . . . crazier than people realize. If we have another summer like last summer, where it rained ninety days in a row, then I'll lose some business. My dad was always trying to get me to go wind surfing when I was growing up. I said, "I don't want to get into one more weather-dependent thing." We sit up here, waiting for the snow to come. And when it does, the wind kicks up to seventy and blows it all over to Troy. It's a constant battle.

(Smiles, shakes his head.) Am I worried? I don't have time to worry about things right now. It's okay, because my wife and my mother worry for me.

Are you into technology and social media?

I think it's interesting how everything is technologically linked, and it's never been harder to get a straight answer out of a person than it is now. I mean, I've got friends who sit inside and play on-line war games all day. They could be in a real world, if they really wanted to. But it's warmer, and more convenient, to sit in their living rooms and play. That kind of concerns me.

You asked how many people have milked a cow, how many people have canned food. If the shit really went down, how many people would not know how to do anything, survival-wise? Not only survival-wise. But just, you know, if someone wasn't cooking their dinner in the microwave for them? Would they know what to do, where to go?

It's staggering how much time people spend on computers and cell phones. They keep talking about getting better cell service in this area. Personally, I don't give a shit. I love the fact I can go to a bar here and there aren't fifty assholes on their cell phones. I'm not resisting technology, but it's really, really changing the world right now. It's pretty scary. The whole global positioning thing . . . it's insane. I can't tell you how many people have been stuck on Route 58 [a local dirt road closed in the winter] because of their GPS. They read their technology but not the signs and crash into a snowbank.

If you had the power to shape something important, something beneficial, in Vermont over the next ten years, what would it be?

That's a tough one. I kind of like what's going on now, which isn't a whole lot of anything. I think that's what draws people here. People do come here to relax. It's a relaxing place. The whole legalized marijuana debate, I really don't care.

What's hard in this town is the loss of young people. You wonder where they all go until you move to a place like Jackson and realize, Everyone's here. Everyone between twenty and thirty is here because they left Vermont. I really don't have an answer how to keep people here. But there's really no younger scene going on in Montgomery. It's all people who moved here when they were my age, when they were young and now are getting older . . . and doing more serious things. I would like to see a younger crowd here.

What about cultural stuff? You have any time to play music?

No. It's something I'd like to get back into. You can never get too old to play music. It's a creative outlet. But I haven't had much time to do anything artistic but work on the cabins, and that inevitably changes into a chore. This project has been my life now for so long that it's hard for me to think of other stuff. But in my personal life experience, it always seems to me that twenty-five to thirty, especially for young men, and women too, is a serious time, in the sense you've kind of outlived your post high-school momentum . . . and what the fuck are you going to do, if anything? It's often a very important transition time.

That's what the other guys I work with in the rental shop are dealing with. They're sitting back and wondering, What in fuck am I going to do? I say, "Well, I know what I'm doing. I got a baby. I got this going on. I work with you assholes. And I got to go wait on a hundred people at Tosca's tonight." In a way it's good to keep your schedule filled, so you don't have those freak outs. You're just too damned busy. But I feel bad for them sometimes. When I talk to this one friend of mine, he really wants to get married and have a baby. But he hasn't found it. I got lucky in that regard. I kind of found that and did it . . . I guess. You got to have some gut instincts. Well, here it is and I'm going to do it. Then you start doing it. Then you learn. ■

Now I can actually get started

Anna Patton

Born: October 4, 1979
Where: Burlington, VT
Siblings: One brother, younger
College: Marlboro College
Degree: Ethnomusicology and comparative literature
Married: No; has a partner
Job: Musician

> Below a rough, natural amphitheater of rock, Anna Patton's home is
> close to the Whetstone Brook a mile or so from downtown Brattleboro.
> She owns the house with Ethan Hazard Watkins, her boyfriend and a
> fiddle player. He's gone when I visit. The woodstove's going, a fan whir-
> ring on top and sending warm air into the kitchen where we sit at the
> table and talk. Anna's from a musical family. Her mother and father still
> play and perform regularly in northern Vermont, but her brother, she
> says, "is a very different kind of musician; he writes and produces pop
> songs in the Philippines for Filipino pop stars."

Growing up in such a family, have you always played an instrument?

I started singing. And played keyboard and recorder. I played a little
bit of French horn, which didn't go that well. Then I took up the clarinet
when I was probably around thirteen. It's a fairly vocal kind of instrument . . . sort of voice-like. I like being able to sing with it. I've actually
been going back to piano lately. It makes me really appreciate being able
to swell a note on the clarinet, because on the piano you kind of hit the
key and you're done. With the clarinet it's all breath, so you can hit a note
and then you can go somewhere with it. It's sort of like the singing voice,
and it works for a lot of different kinds of music.

I don't really know why I chose to play clarinet, other than compared
to the French horn I could use my dexterity. It was very liberating. I feel
fairly wedded to the clarinet.

How many people are in your band?

My main gig is playing for dancing. My band that's working the most
right now is a quintet. It's called Elixir. We have an amazing guitarist
who does percussion and has an octave doubler, so he sounds like he's
playing guitar and percussion at the same time. And there's trumpet and

trombone; the trombonist also calls the dances, so he does double duty. That band mostly flies around.

I got into contra-dance music partly because it was here; I was living in Northampton, and there was a great scene in Greenfield. I liked the dancing, I liked the music. And I didn't have to drive to reach the places. But now, trying to do it for a living, I've kind of ended up in the contra-dance vacation industry. So I really don't play around here with that band all that much. We fly somewhere across the country about twice a month, for a weekend or a week. That's my new job.

Where would you like your music to take you in the next five years?

The dance music is very exciting. It's not that hard to get to the top of the heap because it's this little niche . . . and we're sort of there. So I'd like to keep doing that but I get sick of traveling. I'm always on the lookout for something closer to home where I can make similar money without all the traveling.

People keep going to these weekend dance festivals. Ten years ago there were not very many of these at all, and now there's several going on every weekend in different places in the country. A lot of them are flying New England bands out. For some reason being a New England band is the thing to be. I mean, it's New England music . . . I guess. But I definitely have a long-range goal to not travel so much. It's hard on the body, and I don't like the carbon-footprint aspect of it. It also is a weird thing to have people in California say that what they really need is this Vermont band that plays this sort of grass-roots kind of music. They buy five plane tickets and fly us out there like there's nobody in California who can do the same thing. I feel very ambivalent about that, even while being a hot band.

I'm also getting more into teaching. I have a group that's based in Brattleboro now that plays African, South American, and Balkan instruments. It's a new thing. I'd be interested in doing more concerts, but it's a different circuit. Being a star in the contra-dance world doesn't help very much with getting concert gigs.

Is your community mostly made up of people who play music?

A lot of the people I hang out with are musicians. A lot aren't. One of the things that I like about small-town life is that I can't just break off into a sort of affinity-group world. There just aren't enough people doing one single thing. I have a lot of friends who are teachers and I have some friends who are farmers and into food in various ways. (Anna smiles and laughs.) It's interesting; I have no friends who aren't teachers or farmers or musicians.

Are there many farmer musicians? When Vermont was mostly farmers, there used to be things called kitchen tunks—little music events in the kitchen where people danced.

Oh yeah, with fiddles and things; we do that. But it's hard for a farmer to work professionally because in the folk and traditional music world so much of the work is in the summer. Farmers have to keep their noses to the grindstone in the summer. The music I play, contra-dance music, is really kind of an agricultural tradition. I find it very satisfying when farmers actually come to my gigs.

As an emotional, intellectual, and physical person, which of the three dominate?

Well, to be honest, I'd probably have to say emotional. (Almost begrudgingly, she smiles.) I like to think of myself as an intellectual. I'm both; I think there can be a sort of give and take, heart and brain. I know a lot of people who are pretty intellectual and interested in being very intentional with what they're doing with their lives, and that brings up a lot of somewhat philosophical issues. Some have directed lives. Others don't feel their lives are so directed, but they want them to be. You know, there's an ideological streak. There's a fair amount of seriousness. Most of my friends are also fairly enterprising; they're coming up with projects that are sort of dear to their hearts and going for it. I do think a lot of the people I know my age are taking a lot of things more seriously than our parents did at our ages.

Partly, it's just about how unique the time was when my parents came of age. Maybe it's just the perspective I'm locked into, but I feel it was a pretty special thing to be part of a generation that was throwing so much assumed wisdom out the window and trying so many things and partying so much. I probably have a pretty romantic notion about it. But, you know, maybe if I had been part of that generation instead of mine, I would have still graduated from college and kind of worried about things. It's hard to say what is generational and what is being a free spirit.

You were raised in northern Vermont in Bakersfield. How did you get from there down here, down to Brattleboro?

I came to Brattleboro in 2001. I just picked the town somewhat randomly. I'd spent many years, from sixteen to somewhere in my twenties, touring with Northern Harmony. I'd started home schooling my second year in high school, so I had this flexibility, and I'd go off on these three month tours once or twice a year. Sometimes around the states, sometimes in Europe. After I'd been in Brattleboro about a year I started meeting Marlboro students and decided I would check that out. I'd done three semesters at Smith, then quit.

I got a very typical Marlboro degree: ethnomusicology and comparative literature. And it wasn't until 2006 or 2007 that I got comfortable calling myself a professional musician and stopped wondering when I was going to need a job. Then Ethan and I bought the house in June 2008, sealing the deal, in a way, with Brattleboro and with each other.

So you bought the house together?

Yeah. And that was a big deal for me. When we first went to the bank, they kind of looked at our fairly weird employment and said, "You should apply for a mortgage of this amount." By the time we applied for a mortgage they sort of looked at us again and said, "You do what for a living?" So we ended up at a different bank, and got a co-signing parent. I think that we were able to pay a mortgage, but as far as convincing a bank of that, I don't know if that would have worked out.

In Brattleboro I can definitely call myself a Vermonter; I was born here. That's all it takes in Brattleboro. Growing up in Bakersfield, I really wasn't so sure if I counted as a Vermonter. I think there's things that are a lot easier about living in towns like Brattleboro and even Montpelier with the kids of the hippies and back-to-the-land transplants and musicians.

Does it feel to you that we're in a dark economic time, sort of a dark era?

My sense is that there's a lot less drama about it around here than in larger cities. I haven't noticed a big effect on my work except that people— I play a lot of weddings—people are getting very cheap about them. The scene that I gig in seems to be doing okay so far. I do know people who are unemployed and under employed. It's a little fuzzy around here because it's very cheap to live.

So, you don't need a big nut?

No, you don't need a big nut. Also there's a lot of people who are sort of purposely unemployed or under employed. It's kind of a Brattleboro thing. They kind of piece it together with odd jobs and have artistic projects and make a little money with that. Most of the people I know are sort of in this freelancing, fluctuating employment place.

Let's shift to politics. What do you think of politics here?

I'm not an especially political person, though I try to be aware. Living in Brattleboro, you have to pay attention to what's happening at the Entergy Vermont [nuclear power] plant. A few pretty scary things have happened in the last year. Even people who are pro-nuclear power are looking at it and saying, "This can be done right, but this plant is not doing it right. This particular plant is dangerous." They're now doing this very creepy thing; I need to read more about it. They're kind of selling part of their company, and creating another company that will be able to charge more, and won't have its prices set in the same way. I can't help getting paranoid that this maneuver is them trying to pull something in Brattleboro with this plant.

I pay attention to that, but I'm a little bit more educated about what's going on with food and agriculture, just because I have farmer friends and I'm into the locavore thing. My boyfriend and I kind of like finding our meat in farms around here and growing our vegetables and joining CSAs [Community Supported Agriculture farms]. I think we could do more for small farms. But compared to a lot of places, I think Vermont is an okay place to be a small farmer. I'm glad there's an awareness that there's value to smaller farms and integrated farms in Vermont. Not just an idea that bigger is better.

Are you a Vermont history buff?

Not very much. I pick up some through the kinds of music I'm into. Like I really love traditional Quebecquois music. You research that, you get pictures of northern Vermont, waves of immigration coming in. I remember thinking it was the stupidest thing in the world when we did the history unit in elementary school. Why, why, why are we doing this? I'd be more receptive to it now.

I ask everybody some standard Vermont questions: You ever milk a cow?

No. I've stood by while one was being milked.

Made maple syrup?

I've carried buckets. I don't know how helpful we were. We were kids; we got in a lot of snowball fights.

How about canning food?

It's something I do now. My boyfriend grew up doing it, so he's taught me a little bit.

You fish or hunt?

I've sort of gone fishing; I never caught anything. In northern Vermont,

hunting sort of made sense to me because there's more open land. There's room for it. Down here, I really don't know anyone who hunts, and I don't know where they'd go if they wanted to.

What about winter sports?

A lot of my friends cross country ski. To me, it feels like uphill skiing. Maybe it's embarrassing for me, as a Vermonter, but the last couple of winters I've admitted I don't really love any winter Vermont sports. I've gotten a membership at a pool and go swim. I go on the elliptical machine. I enjoy it a lot.

In this last decade are there things that happened in Vermont that you wished hadn't happened?

That's a funny question. Historical momentum is what it is. It's hard to imagine it kind of swerving. The introduction of civil unions and the backlash was really nasty and bitter and disheartening to my feelings about the state. But I guess being one of the first states to do that, I really don't know how it could have been easier. And then, so many years later, they bring in a gay marriage bill, and it's no big deal.

What about the future? We're a small state in a big country in a globalized world. What are your concerns about the next five, the next ten years?

(She takes a half minute to think about this.) I guess it's something I look at on a pretty personal level. I just hope that people will be able to keep having the quirky artistic life that I'm able to have. I feel pretty lucky, making a living playing music. And I do it in a way that's sort of independent from institutions and government programs. I just hope it won't get any harder than it is to be self-employed and be able to put together a life where you can be both doing work you want to do and be living in Vermont. I feel Vermont is good at allowing people to live these funny, outside-of-the-box lives, and that's good because there are so many people doing peculiar things out in the hills.

Would you like to see Vermont stay the way it is?

I know there's a lot of very economically depressed parts of the state. Given that, I feel it's pretty naive and irresponsible to be against business growth and new businesses moving in.

I'm just hoping that good, responsible businesses will move in and bring more enterprising ideas. Bring people with ideas that they want to try out and think Vermont is a good place with the right energy. It's very interesting—for the last couple of years, going up to Bakersfield for

Christmas, I've met these farmers my age who either ended up there because they were Flack Farm interns [at an organic farm in Enosburg Falls] or even ski bums on the side. They're selling raw milk and growing organic vegetables. So I hope the state might grow in that way.

One of the things that makes my life work is having low-income health care. Vermont makes it easier for self-employed people to get that than other states. So I'm keeping my eye on that, hoping it won't disappear or get subsumed into something that has a lot more red tape involved. You know, kind of like the bank I got my mortgage from; they'll look at me and I won't fit into their boxes, and I'll lose my insurance.

What do you do that enriches you culturally?

I read. I get *The New Yorker*. Sometimes I read *The New York Times*. I watch *The Daily Show* online. If I ever possibly can, I go to see shows at Sandglass Theatre in Putney. It's a puppet theater and it's totally fascinating. It just blows me away we have people doing that. I think the New England Youth Theatre is really fantastic. I almost back out of gigs sometimes to go to their shows, they're so great. I'm involved with the Vermont Jazz Center in Brattleboro. And I don't have a TV. I don't watch a whole lot of movies.

What about social media?

I'm on Facebook. I do not use it professionally. I've avoided Twitter, so far.

Do you have a favorite quote?

I have one that's been popping into my head because of what we've been talking about. "There is no capital of the world, neither here nor anywhere else." It's Czeslaw Milosz writing about studying in Paris, and these people coming from all these smaller European countries to study in Paris, which was supposed to be the capital of the world. Then kind of realizing in the course of his life that the center of the world mentality comes from the mentality that created the totalitarian state.

Can you briefly summarize what you've accomplished in the last decade?

Well, in the last ten years I shifted from a very indecisive, anything's possible part of my life, when I was sort of in and out of college and not sure where I wanted to go musically and not sure where I wanted to live, and I have kind of pushed through that very seductive, anything's possible phase, and chosen a town, and bought a house, and, you know, with a fair amount of luck ended up in a real great occupation that is very fun and creative. And I have a good relationship.

I think being stuck in that anything's possible world, it's sort of like your hands are tied. Even though it's very freeing to be this kid I was, jumping on Northern Harmony tours, and running off to Europe and living on people's couches or squatting, it's also, kind of like, I couldn't really begin the work that I'm doing now, that I really stand by, musically, in terms of building a life, until I picked a town and got past making some decisions. That's another thing about my generation. We have so many choices. There were too many for me. I think with people like me, there's an expectation that you will sort of go out and study and experience and sample some very diverse things, like you'll study abroad and you'll go to college across the country or you'll live somewhere else. There's a little part of me that felt like deciding to settle in Vermont was letting down that voice in my head that has those expectations. But it was the right thing to do because I made certain choices and that made all the other things that I can explore and learn about and do professionally suddenly become accessible. I can actually get started.

ODDS & ENDS

On being an individual and being involved:

I think people are seeking ways to feel they're part of the same thing. Contra dances bring people together. We run one in Brattleboro. All sorts of people come, and they don't have anything in common, a lot of them. Some of them do. But I think just being in towns that are small enough that when there is something going on all sorts of people show up to it has a community-creating, and maybe even tolerance-building, effect. ∎

A nocturnal, I miss most of the day

Grace Potter

Born: June 20, 1983
Where: Randolph, VT
Siblings: One sister, older; one brother, younger
College: St. Lawrence University (two years; studied film)
Degree: No
Married: No
Job: Musician

> I find Grace in Potterville, a cluster of wooden buildings that her father
> and mother built on a steep hillside in Waitsfield. The song-writing,
> band-leading daughter has converted her dad's old sign-making shop
> into living quarters. She lives here when she's not on the road with her
> band, Grace Potter and the Nocturnals. Once I knock on her private
> quarters, Grace opens the door in her bathrobe, the bed behind her a
> mess. She gives me a big hug. Ten minutes later, she's got herself together
> enough to bring coffee and sweets. She's wearing denim splattered with
> white paint, hair up like a 1930s movie starlet. We sit and talk.

*A number of people say we're in this tough financial era. How do you feel
about it?*

It's been harder. I don't remember the golden glow of a happy economy
because I was in college and scraping by with boxes of spaghetti and bottles
of Yellow Tail wine. For me now, my career trajectory has taken me to a
more successful place. Live music hasn't suffered as much as the record
industry [which did start to recover later in the year]. If I'd sold a million
records in 1999, and then, you know, sold two million in 2002, and all of
a sudden wondered where my record sales went, that would be a different
thing. But that's not how it panned out for me. And I'm glad it didn't.

Who handles all your business stuff?

My management is out in L.A. For years, you know, we did everything
ourselves, back when we were playing at farmers markets, clubs, artshows,
and all over the place.

But it's a good time to be a performing artist.

Yeah. People want to see [performance] for their own experience and
have that visceral thing. There is no such thing as a physical album. It's
very sad, but now it's all digital. It's all, you know, something you keep on

your little device. So the only thing you can really own is the life experience; and that's what we do, primarily. I hope the industry starts selling records again.

In the music business what are the negatives and positives?

It's hard for me to talk about the negatives because they don't come in a solid form. I mean, like, there's the reading of your reviews, which I don't do. So that piece of it I've completely avoided. The only negative I get is maybe having somebody come up to me and say something really rude. That happens, but the higher you rise, the harder your critics become and the more avid your fans become. I haven't experienced too many of those extremes yet.

The pleasure parts are certainly performing. But I always had this sort of death wish to be famous. I mean, even as a young child, I was sort of living in the shadow of my sister, in an enjoyable way because she always cast me in her little plays. But I always wanted to be a star, so the joy of this is that I'm getting to live a dream. You know, it's nothing like what I thought it would be, but it certainly is a magical experience. You get what you wish for sometimes, and I actually did. To be honest, and I don't mean to sound like I'm being coy, the negative things that exist, they exist for a brief moment, and I experience them and they're really tough, but they're usually very personal, and, you know, emotional journeys you have to go through anyways.

Is your band sort of a traveling community?

It's my family. That's where I come from, that's what keeps me planted firmly on the ground. The people around me are, you know, people who knew me when we were slugging it out, carrying all of our own gear and booking our own shows. That experience helped me be the musician I am. I never had the diva complex because there was no time to do that.

When in the arc of your career did the band become your family?

Hmmm . . . pretty quickly because we lived together. When I left St. Lawrence and came back to Waitsfield, the whole band moved in with me. Our rehearsal space was right here, downstairs. We spent so much time together that we certainly grew tired of each other, then got to know each other again and went through all the cycles that brothers and sisters, like a litter of puppies, go through. There's the mean kid; there's the, you know, getting-beat-up-by-your-older-sister-or-brother thing. There's that sibling rivalry, but you have to have those experiences. Now it's been almost eight years since I've known most of the guys, and that's a really big milestone for us. We've gone through every piece of negative energy or any problems that will probably continue to arise. We know every piece of each other, so we're ready for those issues now instead of being bowled over by them and being like, "I can't do this, I quit!"

Could you tell me about your song writing method?

I don't have a particular formula, but I have to be in a certain head space to write a song. I need an inspiration, first of all. I need to feel that something else has happened, usually in the outside world, that has jarred me enough so I need to write about it. And it's not always topical. Sometimes it's just hearing somebody else's song that's really good, and I'm jealous that they wrote a great song. Ah, I've got to beat them! That competitive vibe comes out in me, but the inspiration is always the spark of it. I've been lucky enough to have sort of prolific phases in my life where a lot of songs come out at once.

Do you feel that your lyrics are lyrical?

Actually, I do. When I'm writing, I write in verse. Sometimes I'll write the words before the song, which is kind of backwards for a lot of people. You know, musicians tend to let the music do the talking first . . . and the words kind of settle into the music. For me, I'll get a line. Usually it's only one or two words that really need to fit together somehow. I have to find a way to sort of make the music fit around the verse because it feels . . . it feels I'm overly wordy. A lot of times that was one of my main critiques of myself, when I was listening to my songs. I just have so many words. I'm sooo talky, you know. On this new record [*Grace Potter and the Nocturnals*] I experimented with keeping it very simple. Going more for like, "Girl you really got me now." Boom! That's it.

Like a sixties hit?

Sure. (Tosses her head back, laughs.) Wild thing!

Are you more a physical, intellectual, or emotional person?

Lately, I've been very physical. I did get to the point, when I turned twenty-five, I was seeing pieces of my body not working the way I wanted them to work anymore. I couldn't just stand up and do a back handspring anymore. That really unnerved me, so I challenged myself to become a physical person again. For those cerebral years, and those years when I was writing a lot of songs and kind of stewing in my own tomato sauce, I really felt non-physical. I was okay with that. I loved that time in my life, which

allowed me to write a lot of songs and not be running around and playing frisbee all day. Now I've gotten back to the point that when I'm singing on stage I'm much more physical than I used to be. I'm more comfortable dancing and using my hands and my head. And sort of gesturing. I realize that's a part of my performance and my craft is movement.

I work out every day. Even when we're home, I do sit-ups, push-ups, weights, all that stuff. I have to take a walk somewhere every day. I still haven't gotten back into skiing. There's just too much equipment. You can't keep up with all the gear! I don't want to spend my money on that. If I want to spend my money on anything, it's on a Dior dress, baby! (Laughing again, she falls back on the couch.) Anyway, there's plenty physicality in my life now, which is a change and a shift. I still get tired on stage very quickly, but I dance very hard. It just brings about this electrifying energy. James Brown is my all-time hero of live performance. Some day I'd like to get to that point. It's not about the moves, necessarily, but the spirit you're bringing to the music is so powerful you can't help but look like you're getting electrocuted.

Okay, a little on politics. Are you interested in politics?

(Thinks a moment, concentrating.) I mean, I was at the Inauguration! I was in D.C. the entire week, playing concerts. I was on the campaign trail. We raised hundreds of thousands of dollars for the Obama campaign. So I was really politically current at the time. Then we went back out on the road again, and I completely lost track.

Let's talk a little about history. Are you a Vermont history buff?

I can't say that I am. I don't know a lot about the settlers and all that stuff.

What was your major at St. Lawrence?

Supposedly, it was a self-designed film major. But they didn't have an actual film major there, so I needed to sort of run my own course. And I was *really* into film. I wrote three or four screenplays. I was really into the production side of it and figuring out how you make a film from beginning to end because, more so than music, it's the most collaborative thing you can possibly do. And I love that. But no, I didn't complete it. Though some day I'll finish my degree. Just not yet.

Are you still doing anything with film?

I do! I write treatments. I was just on the phone yesterday. We're going to do this sort of guerilla-style viral video where you shoot in a public place and the band is playing a song. Maybe we're in like a public bathroom, and we're sitting there, and you don't realize you're in a bathroom until suddenly you see stalls opening and stuff like that.

(I recount a story about Bill Monroe, the great bluegrass singer, that should have been on film. My ex-wife, an artist Grace knows, masked Monroe years ago in Nashville. Afterwards, when the two of them went to a Kinko's to make xeroxes of his famous mandolin, Monroe played an impromptu concert for the few lucky folks who happened to be in the store.)

That is wild! That is so funny. It must have been wonderful for those Kinko's people—Oh my God. Kinko's is a big part of my career beginnings. We had to print out own CD covers, and we had to fold and cut them; it was like our own little project world in there, every time we had a new poster to print. We spent *so* much time in there, in the Kinko's across from Nectar's [restaurant in Burlington]. You could look at like our invoices from Kinko's and like retrace the history of this band, I swear to God.

Did you perform a lot at Nectar's?

We did a month or a month-and-a-half residency there, where you played every Tuesday night. [It was in 2005, after lots of smaller shows around Vermont and a month playing at Halverson's, another club in Burlington]. The first Tuesday there were like thirty people. On the second Tuesday the *Burlington Free Press* ran an article and put us on the cover. From that second Tuesday all the way through the next couple months it was packed out the door, people couldn't get in. That was the beginning of it for us, in Vermont.

Just another little aside. Years ago, when a friend of mine in Burlington was putting on groups, one day he said, "You got to come down to Hanover with me. I'm putting on a show, they're pretty good." So I jumped in the car and went down. It was Bruce Springsteen and the E-Street Band at the HOP at Dartmouth. There couldn't have been a hundred people there.

Oh my God! Oh my God! [And for the third time]. Ohhh . . . my . . . God! He played Bonoroo when we were there. If I could still be doing what he's doing at his age. He's still a bigger rock star than anybody. I mean, he moves around on that stage—talk about being physical. They have to have, a lot of bands—you wouldn't want to know this—but a lot of bands, big bands, have their own eighteen-wheeler tractor trailer and you're like, "What's in there?" It's a gym. No, I'm not kidding. Lots of stars have them. I'm sure Bruce has one 'cause: God, I mean, he's the man. Some day I'll have my tractor trailer . . . with my elliptical machine! (Grace giggles like a girl.) Hee hee hee.

I ask these classic Vermont questions of everybody: Have you ever milked a cow?

Yes, I have. And at the von Trapp Farm, I bailed lots of hay.

How about tapping maple trees?

As a child, I did it with buckets.

You ever can or put food by?

To me the canning food thing is a version of what people in Vermont do, but it's not what we do. If you go to a farmers market, you know that any food you buy you're usually going to eat quickly, before it goes bad, or just throw a big party so everybody can eat it.

How about hunting and fishing?

I've done both. I went bow hunting with one of my first boyfriends; that was really awesome. I loved bow hunting. I do not like shooting a gun. I went through the safety course. I went hunting up in Huntington. We did the practice pit—the sand pit, rifle pit, whatever they call it. I still have my Carhartts.

How about fishing?

For me fishing was, oddly enough, sort of a cultural, kid, teenager thing because there were bumper stickers, *I'd rather be phishing.* So I think there was some charm to "phishing" at the time I was a kid. It was kind of a cool thing to do. You'd pack your bowl and go "phishing." Yeah . . . look at the water. I don't even think we had any lines. We were just casting.

How about sledding? You still sled?

Oh my God, I had the best sled run ever this year! I do the practice slope at Mad River, which is highly illegal and completely unsafe. Sledding is like my big outdoor adventure. If I'm going to do anything, it's sledding. I can roll with a piece of plastic, and jump on it. That's cool for me. I can do that. On a Mad River Rocket, of course. See, there was powder at the top of the mountain. By the time we'd reached where it gets really steep on the practice slope, we didn't know that it was like complete ice. A sheet of ice. And a rocket and ice do not go together very well. That was just a couple of weeks ago. I almost killed myself. (Stifled laughter.) It was great.

What would you like to see happen in the Mad River Valley in the next five years?

The big thing for me that has been a marker in my whole life in the

Valley is the fact that there is no traffic light. I would be devastated if a traffic light comes. To me, that's like . . . then it's a big city.

I also think it would be cool to see some of the old things come back, like the Blue Tooth, which was always the place to hang. That sort of heart beat of the Valley has scattered to six or seven other places. When you guys came here as ski bums, there wasn't that sense of "I've got to get a job." It was like, "Where we going tonight?" It would be nice to see a little bit of that come back because the way people describe the way the Blue Tooth used to be, it sounds like something I wouldn't want to miss. Being a nocturnal, I miss most of the day here. By the time I'm getting up and getting ready to go downtown, the post office is already closed.

What are your concerns about America as a whole? Where's America headed?

I think we're going to flounder for another year. It's hard to see the light at the end of the tunnel, but I know it's there. I actually wrote a song about it on my new record. It's called "A Tiny Light." Yeah, we are going to struggle, but I do believe there's success around the corner, a sense of change and not accepting the mediocre, big mall day-to-day lifestyle.

Among just the kids I know, there are so many young people with energy being put specifically towards making things happen. Even kids I know who are going to law school are not going to be lawyers. These are environmental lawyers. There's just too much evidence leading to the fact humankind needs to change dramatically. Their day-to-day lifestyles. Also career paths. I've met way too many kids who aren't disillusioned youth talking about how they're going to change the world. These are realistic people. They're going to do something, each and every one is going to do something. We're just the seed of it.

What do you do culturally? Do you read, paint, like movies?

I hate reading because I'm legally blind.

You're legally blind?

I'm legally blind. I was born legally blind.

Now I remember; you use to have those thick glasses.

I still do.

You can't have laser repair surgery that would do the trick for you?

Yeah, it would. But I'm very superstitious, and I don't want to fuck with fate. I feel like I was born with my lack of vision for a reason. I've grown into the person I am today partly because of my eyes not working

properly. I think it would be asking just too much to have perfect eyesight. I'm content to go around with slightly blurry vision. I don't have contacts in or anything. I just can't see very well. But I paint . . . those are my paintings there. And I love movies. I could watch anything . . . maybe not the Grade B sci-fi. I love writing letters. I love writing and the idea of correspondence, that kind of Jane Austen approach to life. Keeping in touch through epistolary relationships. I think that's kind of a special thing. I have several people that I maintain contact with strictly through letters.

What about computers, social networking?

I'm not very technologically advanced. So I don't know OMG; I don't know how to do that. I'll actually take fifteen minutes to write the proper text in a text message. Computers are not my thing. Even in high school I was trying to get a typewriter club, where all the kids who wrote with typewriters could get extensions on when their papers were due. I didn't have a computer at home, I had a typewriter. Of course, it didn't go very far. I referred to computers as the devil several times. I'm still a little bit of a technophobe.

There's a Gospel quality in some of your lyrics, especially on This is Somewhere. *Do you have a rich spiritual life?*

I don't go to church. I don't have a church or a book I read. I have made my way to services on the road. [A while ago] we were cruising around Chicago and there was an art display going on. As we walked down the hallway, we realized the art gallery was connected to a church and there was a service about to start. We didn't even know what religion we were going to check out. All we knew was that the minister had a projector and a picture of "Starry Starry Night," the painting. We thought, What the hell is this going to be? Like this has got to be interesting. So we went in. It ended up being a Presbyterian Church. And it was the first day of the twelve days of Christmas. It was really a spiritual thing for me. We were in a dark time and the band had been suffering through some illness, so it was a really healing evening. Every once in a while spirituality takes me by surprise. It makes me realize how important it is to pray.

Yeah, everything is going to turn out okay because it was all meant to be; that was really soothing for me that night. I needed to hear that because it was dark. We were in dark times.

Do you adhere to the idea that your life is predestined?

No. But I do believe that everything that happens happens for the best. I just had a conversation on a walk the other day with a friend. It's like, we were saying that the tragic death of young people, which seems so senseless and hurtful and wrong, is the one exception, and we couldn't really make sense of it . . . where a long-term illness that leads to death can be a great release to people. (Stares off into air, thinks a while.) I didn't go to church and listen to gospel music as a kid, but you wouldn't know it because I've absorbed so much of that culture. Specifically, the Southern Baptist sort of approach to praising the Lord. And I love gospel music. I love how Ray Charles took it and sort of put it on its ear and turned a sort of soulful, spiritual song into a very secular experience by just changing the lyrics. The last song on my last record, the song called "Big White Gate," is about getting to heaven. And someone deciding conveniently on their death bed that they all of a sudden believe in Jesus, and they want to be saved. Redemption, salvation, it is sort of the impending sense of that that is a great lyrical source for me. I've tried to save myself. I've gone through everything I'm supposed to go through. But in the end I don't see what it's leading to. And so I give up. (Grace smiles but doesn't laugh.) That fight between heaven and hell is what rock and roll is all about.

ODDS & ENDS

On having cross-generational friends:

Michael Lang, who produced the Woodstock Festival, we met him when we were part of a film they did about Woodstock for the fortieth anniversary. We went to the premiere, and Michael really took a shine to Matt, my drummer. He and Matt wound up in a corner, chatting it up the whole time. Later I said, "Michael, you were so sweet to give Matt all your time. What was all that about?" "I'm so fucking tired of, you know, meeting everybody who's my age who has their Woodstock story. I've heard all that. I'm more interested in what's happening now, and what the youth of today has to offer. And what their interpretation of what this festival meant to them is going to do for the future." He wasn't trying to be exclusive, or rude, to people, but it was just like, at a certain point, people who you keep company with, who all come from the same generation, tend to rotate over the same stories, and you start hearing the same stories over and over again. Then those stories change, not in a good way. Usually, they just kind of Pinnochio out.

On no longer playing "Crazy Parade":

Everybody asks me to play that song. When they hear that song, it's a funny thing how it gets to people how it does. All I was trying to do was paint a picture of the day before the 4th of July, and the Warren 4th of July parade. It's one day. People really shine that day, go out on a limb that day. Life should be like that. Not just that one day, but every day should be, you know, treated with that kind of whimsy. And love. And excitement and zest.

Believe it or not, that's exactly how our life has been, since the day I wrote that song until now. I concur with those lyrics, but it's a bit sentimental and kind of gooey for me now. I hate that I'm living exactly what that song is because I felt, immediately after I wrote it, That's so naive to think that that's the way things are really going to be or that's how life should be. But it really has been. ∎

I have no idea what I'm doing out of bed

Lila Rees

Born: October 2, 1979
Where: Burlington, VT
Siblings: One brother, older
Married: Yes
Job: Tattoo artist

Lila Rees' tattoo shop in downtown Barre is in a former clothing store with a 1950s look, an elevated service area, and a work zone that suggests a dentist's space, complete with drills. Ideas for images of tattoos are everywhere. There are anatomy books for real aficionados of her trade and a book filled with the fabulous work of Hokusai. Not much of a tattoo parlor denizen, I stare at *Death or Glory* inked around a skull. In a hardware case some mouth iron for piercing suggests dumb-bells for elves. I thumb a flip book of girl sayings that include *I have no idea what I'm doing out of bed* and *So many men, so many reasons to sleep alone.* For a few minutes I watch one of Lila's clients, a young guy with needles going in and out of his flesh as the artist gives him a Celtic design on a shoulder. Once he hands over money (*We take cash*, is a conspicuous sign in the service area), I sit with Lila in the work zone and we talk about her having opened Rock City Tattoo in one of Vermont's more down-and-out towns.

We're in this depressed economy. Do you feel this is a dark time?

It's pretty bad, I think. Just judging from last year, when I opened, to this year. It seems that all the people who didn't have jobs last year still don't have jobs now. I don't know if I just got lucky and it was like, Ah, a new tattoo shop in Barre. Now it's just like, I'm old news. Or people just don't have money.

I was jamming for months. You couldn't even talk to me. You had to have an appointment to talk to me. Then it died.

But I was really lucky in the last few months. I got married and my dad bought me a house, which was totally dumb luck. If that house hadn't come into my hands, and I hadn't gotten married with another income, I would not be open right now. (Lila lets go a shrill, bewitching giggle, an element of her dark sense of humor). I don't like to think about it.

What about Barre. Is the city's economy slack?

Barre? When I moved here, I didn't know what the big difference between Montpelier and Barre was . . . until I found out the histories of the two cities. Barre was the blue collar, working class, granite industry. Then that died, for whatever reason. Montpelier, the state house, all the hippie dippy stuff. We have the federal court house, the welfare office. And for some reason the state of Vermont sends all the guys on furlough to live in Barre.

That's why, if you drive from Montpelier to Barre, on Route 302, you see like a million motels. That's where all these guys go who are fresh out of jail, sex offenders. They don't have vehicles. They have to walk to the court house, walk to the welfare office. It really sucks. They're not sending them anywhere else but Barre. I didn't kind of know that. I just sort of thought, Central Vermont, whatever—Barre, Montpelier, it's all the same. But it's *not* the same! (She laughs shrilly.) When I worked in Montpelier for a couple of years, when I decided that I wanted to leave, I asked every single client where are you from. Not one of them said Montpelier. They all said Barre, or Orange, or you know, kind of out there. But ninety percent said Barre. So why not put a shop in Barre?

The customers are definitely . . . they are totally out of this world. I think more so even than in Montpelier. When people come here, they feel so much more at ease. They tell me everything. The stories they tell me, and the stuff I observe—it's pretty bizarre.

How did you start this place? Where'd you get the dough?

When I came here, I called every single bank in Barre. As soon as they said, "What kind of business do you want to open?" and I said, "Tattoo shop," they would immediately tell me, "No way. *No way!*" I saw [a rental prospect in Barre] on Craigslist. And I found out the place was in this building. I immediately loved the building. I loved the entrance way, I loved this space in here, the ceilings. Everything about it was exactly what I wanted. I literally had no money. I had no savings. I just decided I was going to do it.

That's when the big economy crashed [September 2008], when everything was going bad. A bank was not going to give me a twenty-five thousand dollar loan to open a tattoo shop in Barre. I walked in, they'd just laugh at me and say, "Get out of here!" I had basically spent my entire twenties building up my credit. I'd never had a credit card. Yet I had perfect credit. And in this one week window I applied for every credit card I could get, and they all approved me. I traded my vehicle—I had this Audi—because how were we going to build this shop when no one had a truck? I went out and got the truck. I did it to sort of keep ahead of the creditors. They wouldn't be able to trace how much I was borrowing in a week! They need time to kind of digest it, so I basically opened every credit card I could . . . and maxed them out.

Now, that's what's been screwing me. I'm on a credit-card treadmill. I basically shut all my avenues for financial freedom by opening this shop.

So, what's your vision? Where would you like to see your business go?

I'd like it to be a private shop. Appointment only. I want to do two clients a day. Custom work for them. Don't kill myself, working all the time. And I'd like to relocate.

Everybody says it takes five years to get established. Especially as a tattoo-er, it takes time. I would like to sort of end up back in Burlington. The problem is that Burlington is over saturated with shops. It's very competitive. The rents are high. But if I get good enough and people want my services, specifically, I might be able to pull off a small, private shop up that way. I really don't like living in Barre.

Except, well, zoning is a tit here. There's like no zoning. (More laughter, a gushing smile.) When I called, they were like, "Yeah, we got one guy that fills in every other week, for an hour." So that was great. He was like, "You want a permit? I'll give you one right now." All that stuff factors in when you open a business. In Burlington, it's like pulling teeth. Here, it was real laid back. I did have some battles with my landlord, but we sorted that all out.

The other cool thing is that it's real easy to get famous in Barre. Especially if you're me. Everybody knows who I am. I don't know anybody. But everybody knows me! It's kind of a curse and a blessing.

Overall, on a scale of one to ten, what would you say your experience has been opening up Rock City Tattoo?

A ten! I'm open. I can make a living. I do what I want . . . for the most part. The whole part of not making a salary sucks.

It'd be nice having more business, I bet.

It's not even that. It's the credit cards. They were gone, I'd be much

better off. But it had to be done. I never thought in a million years that I'd be able to open my own shop. And the thing that is cool is I did exactly what I wanted. I didn't have to cut corners. I didn't have to, you know . . . it was exactly what I sort of envisioned. If I was to go to the coolest tattoo shop . . . and that's what I turned it into. If I was on the street, I'd be one of those shops with the street people coming in all the time, which I don't want. And it wouldn't have this vibe. So it sucks that it's in here, and my landlord's a prob. But, at the same time, it's the effect of the whole experience. And I wanted it to be an experience for customers. Not just get in, get out, give us your money. Because that's what the shop was like I worked in before.

Now you're living and working here in downtown Barre. And your new husband's deployed or he's in training?

His name is Walter. Wes Walter. He first came in here he had a really bad cover up on his arm. It sucked! You could totally see the old tattoo. He was really shy. I ended up tattooing his elbow first. He had a lot of traditional tattoos, which people around here don't have. They were really cool. So, I thought, Who the hell is this guy?

He's from Indiana. He got accepted at Norwich [University] on a wrestling scholarship. He was like fifth in New England. Then Norwich cut the wrestling program. And he wasn't doing so well there. He kind of hated it. He dropped out. When he enlisted with the [Vermont National] guard, they were like, "You won't deploy." And as soon as he signed up, "You're going to Afghanistan, buddy." He was nineteen! I don't think he had a clue he would be going.

When does he ship out?

Probably, next month. But who knows. It changes all the time. He was going to be a driver. Now he's going to be a gunner. He got screwed.

(Last year, before Wes enlisted, he couldn't find a job in central Vermont, Lila remembers.) Nothing. Nothing! So if it wasn't for this deployment . . . . It sucks, but that's the only reason we have good income.

What makes up your community in Barre? Who do you hang out with?
Nobody.

So where do you go for personal hugs and love and affection?
Nowhere.

You're like the lonely girl in Barre.

(Lila doesn't smile.) I go nowhere. I opened this shop, I didn't know I would have to sacrifice my social life and family. People don't come to Barre to hang out. Nobody wants to drive to Barre. I went to the bars down here, maybe twice. And everybody wants to talk to me about the tattoo shop. I mean, it's cool to drum up business. At the same time, I don't want to have too many drinks and piss someone off. Start drama. You know what, I don't really want any friends in Barre. They're going to want free tattoos. I'm very private here. I want to keep my life private. There's even a rumor going around about me now. How can they make rumors about me? I don't do anything. I have two dogs. I come to work, I go home, I take care of the dogs, I eat dinner, I go to bed. I come back to work. Wes is the only outlet I had, and he's gone.

What about other people your age? How are they doing?

People my age I've known for the last ten years are almost all at dead-end jobs. I mean, they live in Burlington. One friend gives people pills for eleven bucks an hour and works insane, retarded hours. My other friend is thirty; he lives in a one-room apartment in Winooski and he roasts coffee down on Pine Street. They're both single. They can't find boyfriends or girlfriends. They can't find rewarding work. I just didn't want to end up like that. I did not want to be thirty years old, or forty years old, going to bars, trying to meet people, working some dead-end job at the mall.

What do you feel is your biggest strength, being intellectual, emotional, or physical?

Maybe intellectual. Because I have to do everything. From tattoos to cleaning to the website to Facebook and MySpace. My advertising. The design of the shop, the build of it. Every single thing I do. With this job, it's more than just technical ability. You have to be able to talk to people while you're hurting them, and have them enjoy their time here. It's kind of a multi-faceted career.

My accountant said, "Don't hire anybody." But when you do that, you take half the money for every tattoo they do. When I'm busy, and the place is full, like it was today, another body is going to help me. But are they going to steal from you? It's a lot of pressure. I don't like to fail. If I fail here, it's ultimately my fault. I can't blame it on somebody else. And that's what freaks me out. I can't say, "My boss sucks!" It's all on me. (She bends forward and pets her dog, an attentive Doberman pup sitting by her knees, and giggles again.) Hence, me getting married.

What do you know about Vermont history?

The Morgan horse. The Spavin Cure in Enosburg. Lake Champlain. In school we'd go to stupid historic crap which totally bored me.

These are my classic Vermont questions: You ever milk a cow?

I could do it. I haven't had to do it. I worked on a farm a little bit.

You ever tap maple trees, make syrup?

Well, my dad does the sugaring. My dad's uncle had a sugarhouse, and we would go up and check the lines. That type of stuff. It was in Jeffersonville.

How about canning, putting food by?

No, but I want to. I had a garden in Winooski. That was pretty good. Now, where I live: A, I don't have the time; B, my yard is shady.

You hunt or fish?

I grew up fishing. I went vegetarian. My dad used to jack deer when I was growing up.

Let's talk about the future. Are you worried about it?

No, I'm not concerned about the future. If the business fails, my plan is to get pregnant. (The highest pitch laugh of our whole session springs from the back of her throat. Finally, she catches her breath.) Isn't that terrible? That's the Barre coming out in me. But I'm getting older. I've only got a few years left to decide.

But it's what they do, they all get pregnant down here. Have their babies. Don't work. And I could do tattoos right out of my house . . . illegally. I figure the economy can't get any worse. It could, but I'm saying no, *and* I can't get any worse at tattooing. I'm only going to get better, get more clients, get better known—that's sort of how it works in this business. I'm wickedly well rounded. Nowadays, if people see, Hey, you have a tattoo shop, they can just click a button and look at your entire portfolio instantly. So I try to stay on the cutting edge of free advertising. I make videos of people with their tattoos. I'm kind of doing guerilla-warfare advertising. I mean, people are never going to stop getting tattoos. I was joking with my aunt about it. I said, "As long as people keep dying and people keep having babies, people are gonna keep getting tattooed." These are two big reasons people get tattooed: their kids's name, people dying.

What would you like to see happen here that might help you out?

The biggest thing I've been griping about is the closing of stores. There is not a grocery store in Barre. I've got to drive ten or fifteen minutes to go to a grocery store. They opened that hippy-dippy Lace place—that agricultural, community exchange thing. I'm sorry, but half the time they don't have anything in there you need. Just *put* a food store in downtown Barre. Even if it's a little market. Shit, someplace I could just walk to and grab a few things and go home. It would create some jobs. Get some of these people off the street. In summertime everybody makes fun of the people with the baby carriages because they don't have anything to do.

I try to put them to work, man. There's this one kid was comin' in here this summer. I know he has no money. His nineteen-year-old girlfriend already has a toddler, with someone else. She's pregnant with his kid. He wants tattoos! Which is totally insane. I'm like, "Dude, you have no money. So why don't you help us move all my shit to my new house, and I'll give you a free tattoo." So I try to get them off of the street, even though I don't have money to pay them. At least it's giving them something to do other than walk around with the baby stroller and their pit bull. (She shrieks with laughter.) There's no jobs around here! People don't have any extra money. If Barre had more of a downtown, community feeling . . . like Montpelier. There, it's a totally different vibe . . . and it's five miles away. Here it's, like, ugh . . . you know. All we have are two Rent-a-Center places because nobody has any credit. And no grocery store. The whole area is set up so weird.

I mean, just having a grocery store is important. Everything closes at six o'clock here. I don't want to be open until ten o'clock at night. I do cash only. It's only going to take one person to think they're smart and want to rob me. I'm not staying open that late by myself. That's why I've got the dog—even though she would never do anything. And I got a firearm, since I moved to Barre. Yeah, I got a firearm and my dog. I tattoo a lot of the cops in the area, and the one cop was like, "Don't bring your gun to work. Someone's going to steal it." So I just bring the dog.

Are you at all interested in politics?

I was thinking of running for frickin' city council because everybody knows who I am.

Barre has this big thing where they're going to redo the downtown. I go

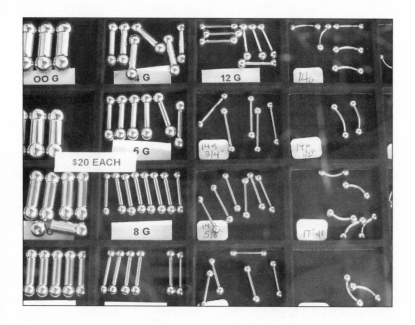

on the *Times-Argus* website at night. I love the reader's comments. It's like the same ten people, with ass-backwards opinions: Barre's never gonna change! You gotta get the scum off the street! Well, yeah, you got to make jobs. It would help if the state stopped sending all the criminals here, for starters. Kind of spread them out a little bit.

Culturally, when you do have free time, what do you do?

I was younger, I used to go out. I'd get tattoos. A lot of dating was going on. Now I've got the dogs that consume my life. I like to take them for hikes. I'm into cooking. When I had more time I was sewing a lot more. I try to paint and make art and stuff, but that's like a job.

(A long, contemplative pause, during which she rubs her dog's head.) Yeah, I was telling Wes, this job has just sucked me dry so much that when I do have free time, I just sort of veg out.

I need to make four grand a month now to stay open. Nothing crazy. Every day I come to work I hope to make two hundred bucks. Some days I can make seven hundred . . . then go a month and only make a grand. So I have to be here even on my day off.

Final question. Where were you when the decade began? What were you doing?

I remember when the year 2000 came and everybody was afraid about Y2K. I was in Boston. I was nineteen. I had to get out of there. I had this weird feeling. I was selling make-up, and I was starting to look into funeral home directing. I was really intrigued with it, doing make-up, because I was a make-up artist. I said to my mom that summer, "Mom, when you die, can I do your make-up?" Like kidding! And she's like, "Oh yeah!" And she like died three months later.

I had to go back to Vermont. I packed my shit in a U-Haul, I drove back home. At the same time they had a job opening at Filene's [in Burlington]. (She'd been working at Filene's in Boston.) It was a pretty good job for somebody twenty. I did the interview and nailed the job. I got settled in and I sort of reconciled my relationship with my mom, which was really bad for a long time. And all of a sudden, she just died at forty-six years old.

She had Graves Disease. It's a thyroid condition. She really didn't tell anybody. She'd gotten real skinny, the doctors wanted to put her on medicine, but it made her fat. She didn't want to take it. And was working seventy hours a week, opening The Hot Topic in the mall. She flew to LA, which I think was part of it because of the altitude change—she'd had some fluid swelling in her legs . . . they were huge! My mom did not have big legs. In retrospect, I felt really guilty afterwards, like I should have known the symptoms. Her thyroid was over active, her heart was pumping really fast all the time. Basically, she had an enlarged heart from pumping and pumping. What happens is all the fluid collects down there in your legs because your body isn't circulating it.

I did do her make-up before the funeral. In the twenty years they'd been open, no one had ever done that before at the funeral home. My family was standing there, totally in shock. I can't believe I did it. I don't know . . . it was kind of cool. We'd already talked about it, which was sort of creepy. I didn't think she was going to die.

I had a real bad relationship with my mom. I always said, "Never get a mom tattoo; I hate my mom." Well, the next day after she died, I was like, I'm going to get a mom tattoo. I went to Body Art and that's where I met Tyree. I kept getting tattooed by Tyree. After a couple years, he offered me an apprenticeship. I didn't think I could tattoo. He said, "You want to learn?" And I said, "No." (She laughs.) I told him no! Then I started thinking about it, and I'm like, I watch all these people come in with portfolios and artwork, begging for an apprenticeship. I might as well try it. What is the worst that is going to happen?

For me, everything sort of happened the way it was supposed to for ten years. It all sort of worked out. ■

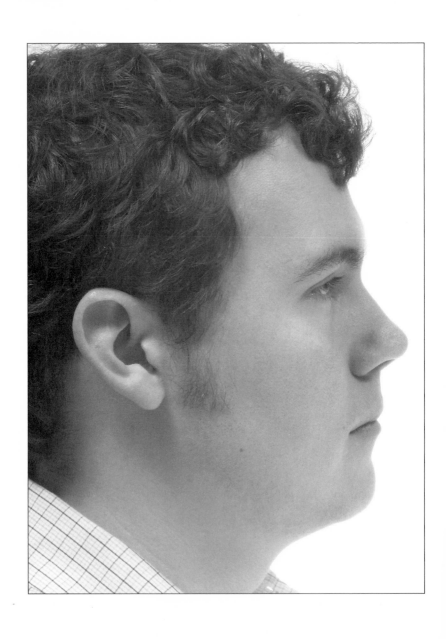

The economy's not working for us

Colin Robinson

Born: January 1, 1984
Where: Brattleboro, VT
Siblings: "I'm an only child."
College: University of Vermont
Degree: Cultural Anthropology
Married: Yes
Job: Director of Policy and Advocacy/Peace and Justice Center

"I was the first boy born in Vermont in 1984," Colin tells me when we meet at the Peace and Justice Center store by the waterfront in Burlington. He seems pretty happy about that, so I say, "They didn't name you Orwell?" He shakes his head and laughs, says that twin girls born in Randolph minutes before him knocked him out of Vermont's first baby competition for that auspicious year. Maybe so, but the George Orwell linkage proves a sound one. It quickly becomes clear that Colin Robinson is a political justice crusader in a time when both economic data and vocal critics say that policy and regulations favor the rich and protect corporations while many regular people, including Vermonters, "play by the rules, do everything they've always been told to do, and can't meet their basic needs."

What do you think of the economic realities in Vermont and in America?

Without a doubt we're in the worst economic climate since the Great Depression. The most unfortunate component [of this situation] is that the narrative around it has focused on blaming George Bush or the housing "bubble" that burst. Based on the work we've been doing here at Peace and Justice, and on what the data shows, it's something that's been in the making for over forty years.

Over that period there's been a gradual and persistent decline in real wages. The dollar reached its peak value for the average American, and average Vermonter, in 1968; if the minimum wage had kept up with inflation, it would be over ten dollars an hour now. Over the last thirty years we also saw a massive tax shift from those who could afford to pay, the wealthy in our society, to those who couldn't . . . and can't to this day. Pensions, solid health care plans [are now often funded by] employee contributions. We're shifting from pensions to 401k's, from good health care to health savings accounts; they take money out of the pockets of the vast majority of us. Right here in Vermont it's trended the exact same way. The folks that have done the best are the top five percent in terms of wage earners, and the lowest twenty percent have seen a decline.

Are you saying that Vermont is more in lockstep with the rest of America economically than it was in the past?

That's exactly it. I mean, we're part of a big nation that interacts with the world. That being said, I think historically—and this is borne out in the current economics—the massive fluctuations, the massive sways in economic trends, they don't impact Vermont quite as strongly. Our highs aren't quite as high and our lows aren't quite as low. Vermonters have that Yankee sensibility, that Yankee work ethic; they've always been a common sense people. So they're less prone to, you know, gimmicky or sound-bite issue politics.

We talk to a lot of people who are low-wage Vermonters, who are often multi-generational Vermonters, often multi-generational Vermonters who have been in poverty. They're salt-of-the-earth folk who don't want to have a big fancy house, but do want to be able to put food on their table. They understand the issues because they're dealing with them every day.

I think one thing that makes Vermont unique is this: Folks here *really* do think. They take the time to step back and say, "Okay, what's going to be best for my family? What's going to be the best for me and my family to meet our basic needs? And what do we need to get there?" Are there folks in Vermont who vote against their own self-interest? Of course. But generally, many of them understand on a visceral level that the economy isn't working for them. They're working forty, sixty hours a week . . . one or two jobs . . . and something continually isn't working. They know it has nothing to do with whether or not someone's pro-life or pro-choice. It has nothing to do with whether same sex marriage couples can get married or not. They understand that it has to do with the fact that their jobs are paying them wages that don't allow them to meet their basic needs.

I think working people sort of understand that the factors that created this financial mess are in many ways beyond them. That's not to say it's beyond their control, because the economy is the way it is because we all agree to participate in a system that does not work for most people.

But they've sort of recognized the need for a livable wage. That's hitting home for a lot of people.

What's been interesting at a political level in Vermont—and I see this

nationally as well—is policy makers running towards and putting more emphasis on the concerns of businesses. [Meanwhile], the costs of child care, housing, and health care are crushing Vermont family budgets. They're also crushing Vermont business budgets. If we can bring the costs down for both groups, then Vermont businesses will be able to thrive and regular working folks will be able to thrive.

Which of the issues—a livable wage, better working conditions, health care—do you think can realistically be impacted by your efforts over the next four or five years?

There needs to be a comprehensive approach. Bringing up the minimum wage is really only half the problem. The other half is the cost drivers. But more important is Vermont's dependence on imports. To address some of the issues, the answer is Vermonters supporting Vermonters, investing in Vermonters, and, you know, keeping more of our money in Vermont. There's been movement in that direction, especially in the food and agricultural sectors. We know we've made progress in food. But what about energy—creating more opportunity for small-scale hydro-electric in Vermont? That was the bedrock of production in Vermont a hundred years ago. By shifting the emphasis back to investing in Vermonters, investing in our neighbors, we reduce costs and keep money here. That allows us to create a more equitable economy.

What pisses you off, what makes you angry about these inequities we're discussing?

What gets me more than anything is there are large institutions in this state, and companies, that pay their employees horrible wages. That just seems to me to be so fundamentally wrong in the richest country on earth. We have childhood hunger, we have affordable-housing crunches to no end, we have people who can't get from one place to another because we have no public transportation infrastructure.

Public transit, like so many public systems, was systematically dismantled. For instance, I know that a train used to run between Putney and Brattleboro six times a day. People commuted on the train. It's one of those things that would be wonderful to do now, but they stopped doing it in 1954. You could go from Brattleboro to New York City faster in the early 1930s than you can in 2010. In Burlington there used to be street cars but they were bought up by Vermont Transit, the bus company. They said, "Well, we want buses to be king." They tore up the tracks. The famous last car was set on fire up at the top of Main Street by UVM and run down the tracks on the hill right into Lake Champlain.

How does the Peace and Justice pay its bills?

Money has been tight. But we have an incredible membership base, and they've helped us weather this economic storm. We've been around and survived for thirty-one years. We've survived doing work that most of the powers-that-be don't want us to be doing. Our store has always provided considerable cash flow. When grants and donations are lean, the store has helped us pay the bills.

Let's talk about Vermont politics. Which parts of state government do you lobby to cooperate with your efforts?

We work with the legislature, using both inside and outside strategies. Every week we're down there in Montpelier. You have to have relationships on the inside. At the same time you also have to be on the outside, agitating and mobilizing people. We've never felt comfortable with the belief that the way change happens is to just be on the inside, playing the game. We work hard to get local folks to talk to politicians, to talk at Town Meetings. One of the best assets that we have in Vermont is that our legislature is a citizens' legislature. People know their lawmakers because they're their neighbors, they own the country store, they're their electrician. That's pretty unique. We try to use it to our advantage when working on issues in Montpelier.

We also make sure our work is founded on sound economic research. We say, "You've got to look at the data." Too often decisions are made not looking at the numbers. For instance, we hear across the board, "Vermont is bad for business; Vermont is pushing business away; this is an atrocious place for business to grow." That's all you hear! Nobody ever looked at the data. So we said, "Let's look at the data; let's compare Vermont to all fifty states and see if this is actually true." And what we found is, it's not.

What about your personal community these days?

I live in Winooski. I'm married. My wife grew up in Guilford; we've been together since we were both sixteen. We met in a high school social studies class in Brattleboro. We bought our house here about two years ago with the help of the Champlain Housing Trust, which was a godsend; we wouldn't have been able to buy a house without them.

My community, in a lot of ways, is made up of other people working on the same types of issues I work on. But without a doubt my best friends are friends I've met in random ways. (He smiles.) We're just friends because we're friends! We have common interests and political beliefs but that's not the backbone of the friendships.

Do you consider yourself mostly a physical, intellectual, or emotional person?
Hmm . . . (makes a tapping sound with tongue as he thinks) . . . I'm
probably an intellectual person with a smaller emotional side. I feel that
I'm somebody who has a tremendous amount of empathy for people, and
a lot of the issues that I'm passionate about and I work on, I come to from
a very emotional place. With a sense of injustice that is very deeply rooted.
At the same time I think a lot about issues and really enjoy conversation
and debate.
This sense of injustice you feel, where does it come from?
In part it comes from my youth and my parents. You know, I would
never describe them as activists, but they were always sort of progressively
minded. I do remember hearing stories about their parents. I remember
my dad telling me that his parents, when he was eleven, brought him to
the march on Washington in 1963. At eleven, he saw Martin Luther King's
"I Have a Dream" speech. He told me stories about getting hate calls on
the north shore of Massachusetts, being called, "Nigger lover." You know,
I think that those stories were the initial seeds.

In high school I had a teacher that really taught me to think and gave me the tools to analyze and be critical of issues. He was a social studies teacher by the name of Tim Kipp at Brattleboro Union High School. I helped start a group there called Child Labor Education in Action. High school students, we were saying, "There are people our age around the world who can't go to school because they have to work for pennies to make Nike shoes." That was where my class consciousness started coming out. I started understanding the economic inequities, class components, and most importantly, power and the effect it has on the democratic process.

Are you a Vermont history buff?

I definitely am. I wish I'd taken more history classes. At UVM there's a whole section on Vermont studies, and I never took any of the classes. I totally regret it. But lately I've read a lot more books on Vermont history and have grown to appreciate my home state a lot more.

Look at some of the things that were happening in the first half of the twentieth century, with rural electrification, with infrastructure investments, with the fact that the first Social Security recipient was a woman from Ludlow in 1939. I recently saw something that showed that a lot of the same conversations we're having now—how to use state resources, how to invest in the public good, how to make sure Vermonters are meeting their basic needs—these were conversations that Vermonters were having seventy-five years ago. There were studies done back then, saying, This is what we need to do to make sure all Vermonters can put food on the table.

There are also two things that, if they had not happened, would have made the state a very different place. One was the reapportionment of the Vermont legislature in 1964. Each town used to have a representative, you know; it's totally fascinating. It's a piece of Vermont history I only read about recently. If we still lived in a system where Burlington had the same one vote in the House that Jamaica does, or Montgomery does, it would be different. The other big thing is Act 250. [Vermont's land development act, passed in 1970, was the first major environmental control law in America]. Literally, the landscape of Vermont could look totally differently if Act 250 hadn't passed.

I don't know if it was part of Act 250 [it wasn't], but simple things like the fact we don't have billboards in Vermont are historic. (Colin speaks in a low, sort of conspiratorial tone.) A friend of mine had this interview for a job he was applying for, and they asked him, "We know there are no billboards in Vermont, but if you had to have one billboard and you could put anything on it, What would it be?" His answer, I just thought was brilliant. He said, "I'd make it look like the trees behind it so you couldn't even tell it was there."

Could you give me a summary of what you've accomplished over the last decade?

I've been a persistent organizer, advocate, and agitator for issues of economic injustice in Vermont. My trajectory after high school was going to UVM, helping to found the Student Labor Action Project [an attempt to get livable wages for all employees at the university]. My past decade has been educating Vermonters and organizing Vermonters, and getting them to agitate for political and economic equity in the state.

That said, my perspectives have changed. I've recognized that doing organizing work that demands you work eighty to one hundred hours a week is incredibly, fundamentally important work . . . and I've recognized it's *not* the work for me. That's one of the things that's changed. I've also gotten a better sense for where my skills and interests converge, and where I can be the most effective collaborating with others working in ways that they can be most effective. The reality is that any changes on any of these issues are only going to happen when you have people with diverse skills and knowledge working in complementary ways.

What are your concerns about the future in Vermont over the next five years?

On a personal level I think we've got to do something about health care. Nationally, change is only going to get us halfway there. Vermont can lead the nation in creating a health-care system that works for everybody. Our energy future, and energy infrastructure, is tremendously important. But we shouldn't be bogged down in the permitting process. For instance, the process for hydro dams in Vermont is ridiculous, absolutely insane. If we're serious, we need to do something about that.

I think another one you're seeing come to a head now in Vermont is our concern for local control in education. You know, the Vermont constitution guarantees every citizen the right to an education. It's an amazing clause. If we're serious about investing in the future, and the future is the children of Vermont, then we need to make sure our schools are teaching kids the best they possibly can. I think that will lead towards some consolidation . . . eventually. We need to get to an openness to having that conversation; now there's a lot of resistance.

I'm going to ask you my classic Vermont questions: You ever milked a cow?
Never.

Ever made maple syrup?
Drilled holes, boiled in Putney when I was a kid.

You ever put food by? Can food?
We've canned some. Not a whole lot. We have a garden.

What about hunting and fishing?
I've never hunted. I've done some fly fishing, and regular rod-and-reel.

Winter sports? You ski, snowboard?
You know, I grew up skiing like a lot of Vermonters. Skiing was made affordable for me as a youth, and then was made unaffordable for me as an adult. Now, as a native Vermonter who grew up skiing and loves to ski, I can't really afford to ski.

Cultural questions: You a movie goer, you like to read?
I'm a big fan of movies and read a lot. I read all the major newspapers in Vermont—at least peruse them online—along with the *New York Times*. For a long time I read a lot of non-fiction related to my work. Then I realized that was just too much. (Laughs self-mockingly.) This last summer I discovered the mystery novel. Escapist reading . . . totally.

How much do you use social media?
Organizationally, we're trying to use it a lot more, mostly Facebook and Twitter, trying to integrate it a lot more with what we do. Personally, I'm on Facebook at least once a day. I don't do Twitter. I'm on my email all the time; I never log out. And I got an iPhone this summer. My wife and I have become even more addicted now that we have iPhones and they're always burning in our pockets.

Do you reflect at all on whether technology has enslaved or liberated us?
I've thought about it. For all its benefits, and I think it does have benefits, I do have serious concerns about technology's impact on community. I don't think there is anything that can ever replace the face-to-face connections: neighbor to neighbor, friend to friend, family to family. That's been a fundamental part of being human, and making us human. There's almost nothing more fundamental to being a human than that. I do fear that the isolation of technology is taking away from some of those intimate personal connections. ∎

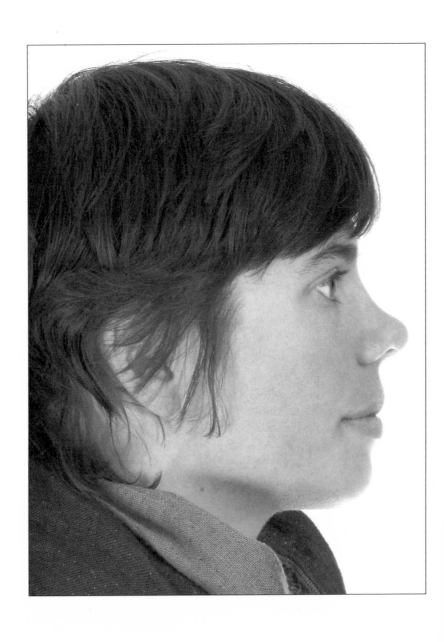

I've got to keep us moving forward

Katherine Sims

Born: November 5, 1981
Where: Wellesley, MA
Siblings: One brother, younger
College: Yale University
Degree: Art History
Married: Yes
Job: Founder and Director of Green Mountain Farm-to-School

> The Green Mountain Farm-to-School program has its offices on Main
> Street in Newport, Vermont. I meet Katherine Sims there, in a bare
> room, and the voluble founder of the program, which now supplies
> twenty-odd schools in northeast Vermont with raw foods from local
> producers, talks fast. She reels off facts and details and the odd quirky
> bit, like the fact that her birthday is on Guy Fawkes Day in England
> ("He's the guy who tried to blow up Parliament") and that art history at
> Yale was a major through which you could examine anything, from the
> environment to women's issues. She starts to explain how the farms-to-
> school program works, and I ask her to back up and fill me in on the real
> beginnings: her. I ask how a suburban preppie who went to Yale ended
> up in the Northeast Kingdom with her hands in the dirt?

It all started with food. I grew up as an athlete to full-time working parents.
We ate dinner together. There was a lot of white food: white potatoes,
white pasta. But I took a semester off—I had a language requirement and
languages aren't really my thing. I took six weeks and went to Florence
and tried to bone up on speaking Italian. That was really my first exposure
to communities that really valued food, and it really sort of awakened my
taste buds.

When I came back [to Yale], I just needed to learn more about food. I
found I could get really good food like I had in Italy right in Connecticut,
at a neighboring farm. I started volunteering on weekends and discovered,
Wow, now not only am I walking back home with bushels of awesome
tomatoes, but I'm really enjoying the work, too. It was fun to stick my
hands in the dirt, and to be outside in the sun, and experience and sort
of learn hands-on. So then I quit the soccer team, and I backed off from

other sports and was able to take a semester off from school and came up to Vermont to learn more about farming.

Vermont was always kind of a special place. My dad grew up in South Burlington, my grandparents lived there. Our family is apparently descended from Ethan Allen, so we have long roots. I had some of my first gardening memories in my grandmother's garden up in Vermont, taking out rhubarb and leeks. My mum went to Middlebury College and my parents met at UVM, taking post-grad courses. So it was like, Yeah, I want to learn about farming more intensively and Vermont's the place to do it.

I got a list of the Vermont farms where apprenticeships were available and called one farm and it was like January and they were like, "We won't be very busy, but call Jack and Anne Lazor, Butterworks Farm." I called them and they were like, "Can you start tomorrow?"

It was just a perfect fit because the Lazors are such innovators, and they've been doing so much for agriculture in Vermont. And they're famous. Every day exciting people would be stopping by. I got introduced to so many great Vermont farm and food folks. I got to learn about milking and value-added products and growing beans, sunflowers, and greens. I got hooked on Westfield and the area and on food and farming. I also worked at Lazy Lady Farm in Westfield, and Berry Creek Farm, to learn about goat, dairy and cheese making and vegetable farming. Then I went back to school.

And back at Yale, you started a farm?

Yeah. Right now it's a one-acre farm that undergraduates can work on as interns. They've tried to make it grow into this initiative that has staff. School groups come and visit, and they try to integrate agriculture and agrarian studies into the curriculum as part of graduate and under-graduate programs.

They even have a food-and-farm colloquium. And sort of piloted a program at the white elementary school right in New Haven and rebuilt three or four raised beds with the kids and started gardening right in the courtyard there. That was amazing for me to see. It was the first time I got to witness the power of putting a seed in the ground and watching things grow and see we could really inspire and excite young kids to make healthy food choices.

It seems our program is a bright light in the economy of the Northeast Kingdom? How'd you get it up and running?

Green Mountain Farm-to-School started as a pilot program in the Jay/ Westfield joint elementary school. Anne Lazor was on the school board and knew the school had a garden in the past and was maybe interested in having a garden program. We created year-round, after-school, gardening-cooking programs where students are planting seeds, designing a garden that's growing food for the cafeteria, and then, in the winter, kids are learning where the food comes from and cooking in the cafeteria. After a year of running that program, there was enthusiasm at the district level to secure some funding. So I started working to serve other schools in the area. This spring we're actually building five more gardens, and we'll be at twenty schools. Our furthest south is in Cambridge. It's all about each community sort of creating its own network of food system and education.

What about the farmers? Are you giving small, organic producers a new life line?

We are making the case for that. I don't think anyone's quitting their day job to sell just to schools. We just started partnerships with senior meal sites as well. I think there's a great potential to be serving larger institutional purchasers, like Jay Peak, and hospitals.

Hospitals? You're going to make hospital food better?

(She laughs.) I mean, it's a surprising concept: we're going to heal ourselves by visiting a doctor and eating great food. It's ridiculous, but it's easier to get a head of lettuce from California sometimes than it is from your neighbor down the road.

Everything seems to have gone forward almost unbelievably smoothly.

(Smiles tolerantly.) Ask my husband if I ever go home anymore.

What does your husband do?

A little bit of everything. He's a beekeeper and markets his organic honey all across the Northeast in the natural-food stores of Vermont. And he's also a builder. We do some homesteading, like penned sheep and a draft horse. We have forty acres in Westfield and manage another twenty in hay.

This might be a good time for me to ask my classic Vermont questions: Have you ever milked a cow?

Yeah. I've milked goats, too.

You ever make maple syrup?

At Kingdom Mountain Maple. And when I lived at Butterworks I tapped a couple trees myself. That's actually how I met my husband. I had a pan that needed to be soldered together a little bit. It had a hole. He was

the man to do it. I would say that Jack and Anna Lazor were the reason I was drawn to Vermont, and Josh is the reason I stayed.

Putting food by, do you do that?

That's my Bible. I do green beans and tomatoes . . . beets and salsa . . . blackberry jam. That's one of my favorite parts of our house, the pantry downstairs with all the Mason jars. We live off grid. All solar. We'd like to have a root cellar.

How about hunting and fishing?

Josh got an eight-point buck in our front yard. We were, actually, both vegetarian for a long time. Then started eating meat. It was venison from Pennsylvania that his dad brought us.

I've shot guns and go fishing in Lake Champlain for bass and perch and something they call crappy.

Any winter sports?

It snows I ski. I telemark and do some back-country.

You do any snowshoeing or skating?

No, I like to go fast.

I have another question about your work. Is there some aspect of it that irritates you? Usually there's a burr under even the nicest of saddles.

(Half joking) Are you trying to draw out some challenges for me? I have to maintain a positive focus to keep us moving forwards.

It is hard not to be frustrated over the whole industrial agricultural food system. I mean, we've put up such a giant system that's focused on profit and consolidation, where food is made just as quickly and simply and cheaply as possible. It's so easy to get excited about growing food with kids at their school, but sometimes I feel like the impact we're having is just like this drop in a giant pond. Do we really have what it takes to undo this enormous system? Processed food is yummy; our taste buds go wild and it's so cheap. It's a lot to change. Real good local food tastes good and is so much more meaningful when we eat it and consume it, but I understand why we've headed in a different direction. To turn our whole culture around, I hope that we're not too late to do that.

I think [the recession has] made me continue to underscore the importance of what we're doing with kids in local schools. The numbers are pretty staggering. We know more and more students that we work with at schools are hungry, so we can help to get fresh local food into our school cafeterias where they're serving breakfast and lunch. I think that just adds greater importance to the work we're doing that helps people to learn how to make healthy choices on minimum budgets. And especially when folks that are making cutbacks at home, the cheapest foods are often the ones that are the least healthy for us.

In your private time, when you're lying in bed and contemplating your destiny, do you feel you're more of an intellectual person, an emotional person, or a physical person?

Can I be all three? For me, I've had a real evolution . . . growing up and going to private school, and, you know, an Ivy League college with a real focus on professional, academic, intellectual life. My mom has been asking me for a long time what I'm doing. (Laughs) But I've felt a really personal connection to the work of farming and homesteading, producing the fuel for our life. And I sort of pulled back from the intellectual life and committed myself. You know, my husband and I are building a house together in Westfield—it was really personally satisfying, but it didn't feel quite enough for me. It's been exciting to sort of marry my interest in the agrarian lifestyle with my focus and experience in building systems and model programs. To take what's satisfying for me personally and bring that to a larger community.

What are you concerns for the near future? What would you like to see happen in Vermont over the next five to ten years?

I'm concerned that the work we and the other organizations are doing around food and farming won't be enough and that the obesity rates will continue to skyrocket and the cost of health care will continue to skyrocket and that we won't have a next generation of farmers. It will be too expensive to buy land and there won't be enough land available. So my vision would be that our whole culture makes a shift and values where food comes from. And people cook and eat together and buy food from their neighbors who can afford to farm because there's support from a community.

What about land buying? It's a real issue, the price of property. Almost everybody I've interviewed has talked about this. What's going on to alleviate high prices?

I've heard of two or three folks who were able to partner with landowners and slowly transition property. I think that's a great model for our dairy farmers to partner with younger farmers. But coming up with all that capital, this is a real barrier for a lot of people.

Do you think one of the opportunities is turning our large, thousand-cow farms into producers of other products?

Absolutely. You can take those giant farms and turn them into multi-farm enterprises. You know, right now, schools are not buying all local, but if they were the challenge becomes having enough supply. The state has an incredible demand if you include hospitals and prisons, schools, and other large institutions buying local. That's a lot of food. The question is, Do we have enough farmers and land available to produce all the potatoes that you need to feed our community? But that's a problem I'd love to have. It'll be great when we don't have enough Vermont apples to sustain ourselves.

What about other things? Are you worried about the weather? Are you worried about the fact that Vermont's the 49th oldest state per capita and has an aging problem?

An age-imbalanced Vermont will be quite a tax burden. And I am really worried about the weather. I try to not think about that because I don't have answers. I'm trying not to think that it's just a coincidence that we've had so many earthquakes and giants hurricanes and no snow . . . earlier and earlier sugaring seasons that aren't as good . . . longer and longer falls. I guess, on one hand, it'll help me to grow more tomatoes and peppers.

Yeah, if new bugs don't kill them all. With warmer weather Vermont could become a place that is more attractive for a large number of people.

That would not necessarily be good either.

Most of your contemporaries I've talked to, they want Vermont to change but they don't want the population to grow a lot.

It's like, I want to buy some land and put a house on it but no one else can do that. It's a tricky balance. Newport and Lake Memphremagog are a great example of a wonderful, thriving, sort of small city environment. I think it would be a shame if the renaissance that I expect to see pushes out our current community. I don't know what the answer is, how to do growth in a way that preserves our character, values what's important to us, improves it but without losing what's special, without overrunning our population.

Do you find, when you drive around Vermont, that most people don't even know where Newport is?

Oh, absolutely.

A few cultural questions. Are you a movie lover, read a lot, listen to music?

Thank God for Netflix! I mean, the general store is great, but I can only

watch so many grade-B new releases. We play games: cribbage, ping-pong, backgammon, dominoes, Set. I've been on a Queen Elizabeth I kick. I've watched every old historic movie about Queen Elizabeth I there was. I'm reading her biography. VPR's another lifeline.

What role does social media play in your life?

It has more of a life in our organization. We have a Facebook page and a Twitter page. A younger staff member [takes care of it]. I was really skeptical at first, like, This is gonna take way too much time, I don't see anyone in the Kingdom even using it. But it's been incredible, some of the interactions we've had with people who wouldn't be interacting with us in any other way. And being able to watch what people spread of our message and to learn more from other people—it's actually pretty cool.

I mean, as long as it doesn't prevent us from being in the real world, too. And doing real work.

I do have an iPhone.

You're off the grid and have an iPhone?

It's funny . . . a new version of the back-to-the-lander. I struggle with that.

Do you have a favorite quote?

Wendell Berry's "Eating is an agricultural act." (Pause) I'm sooo single-minded. ∎

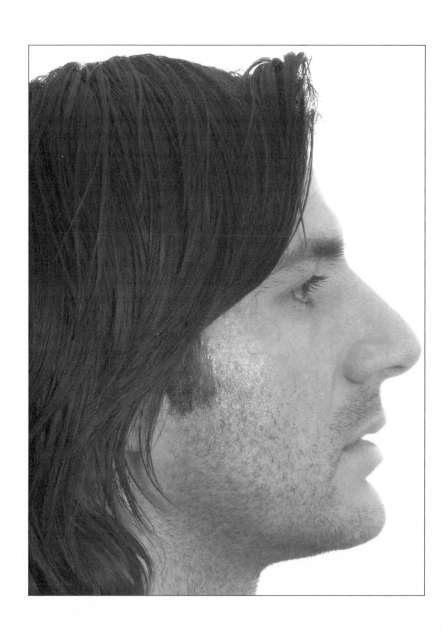

I'm sort of a gladiator

George Spaneas

Born: November 21, 1972
Where: Attleboro, MA
Siblings: One brother, older
College: Marshall University, John Marshall Law School
Degrees: Psychology, Law
Married: No
Job: Trial lawyer

> To me, the most remarkable thing about George Spaneas is that he
> looks *so* not like an attorney. Unshaven, thick dark long hair. No suit,
> no collared shirt even. The sole clue he's a lawyer sets on his otherwise
> bare desk in his office at Clauson, Atwood & Spaneas. It's the scales
> of justice. George does have college degrees on the wall and a couple
> touristy pictures of Greece and the deep-blue Mediterranean. He's soon
> holding up another photograph, though—this one of a man in uniform
> in Greece in the early 1930s—and tells me a seminal story of his family's
> past. It's a story in which his grandfather, for whom George is named,
> was killed in a vendetta, setting off a long string of events that led his
> parents to America and George to Vermont where he became a trial
> lawyer because, as he puts it, "It was just meant to be."

Tell me about your grandfather. What happened to him?

I've always had this very strong connection to my grandfather, though
I never met him, never knew him. He was murdered when my father was
an infant. There was a vendetta in his village over a piece of property that
the community used to graze sheep on. One family decided that they were
going to take that piece of property over and claim it as their own. So my
grandfather, who was sort of the mayor or the selectman of the town, took
it on himself to say, "That's not going to happen. This family's not taking
over this property; it's going to stay for everybody." That was the dispute.
He argued with this other family for a while; I think it got physical at some
of the meetings. Nobody shot anybody, but they all carried guns. Then this
family that wanted to take over the property discovered that my grandfather was going to be traveling to a neighboring town. A person from the
other family hid behind a stone wall, and as my grandfather passed, he
shot him in the back three or four times.

We're talking the 1930s. My father was born in 1933; my father was just a couple months old when it happened. There was like a civil war. During that time in Greece, it was very bloody. My mother grew up in a place in northern Greece; they were very poor. Her mother got murdered by militants or communists who were after her father; they couldn't capture her father, so instead they took her mother, brought her to the mountains and murdered her. My mother was raised by her grandmother.

So there were murders on both sides of your family during your grandparents' time?

Yes. Communism was spreading; there was a battle between communism and democracy going on. [During World War II] Greece was on the Axis side. My father remembers, as a child, seeing German soldiers walking through. Then my father and mother moved to America in the 1950s. For my mother, it was the American dream to have a better life. To raise a family in a better world, a better place.

How did you get to Vermont?

In 1988 my parents bought land in South Strafford. I was sixteen. I fell in love with the place. I chose Hanover High School because I met a couple kids from South Strafford at Coburn's Store in town. They played football at Hanover. I got rides with them back and forth. It was rough. I had to walk up and down essentially a mountain to go sleep where we were living until our house got built. We lived in a small camp, with an outdoor shower.

So you played football in high school?

Yeah. I played tailback and strong safety. Athletics were not very big in my family; football wasn't something I learned from my mother or father. When football used to come on in my house, I remember, as a kid, we used to change the channel. "What is this game . . . everybody smashing each other?"

It was just sort of accidental how I got into it. I used to walk to grade school [in Attleboro, MA], and I had a friend. We used to play before class. He was involved in a game in the parking lot and I wanted to hang around with him, so I kind of injected myself into the game. I just ran with everybody else, and as I ran, I ran really fast, and the next thing I knew there was a ball in the air and it ended up in my hands. I caught it, reached up and grabbed it. It was a touchdown and all the kids were like hugging me and slapping me high fives, and I was like, Wow, what a great feeling!

Man, I'm *good* at something. I'm fast, I can run. So I kept at it and I just started dominating. My God, I'm good at this sport! That's how I got into football. It was just like that, just accidental in the parking lot.

At Hanover High our team did well. My junior year we won seven or eight games. My senior year we made it to the state semi-finals. I don't ever remember, from the time I was eight years old and started football until the time I finished, not being on a successful football team.

Did you play in the Shrine Game [an annual Vermont versus New Hampshire contest played by all-star players from both states]?

Yeah. It was at Dartmouth on a natural grass field. I think we had about ten thousand spectators. The papers made a big deal about me being a Vermonter and running wild for New Hampshire because I was playing running back.

You're not that big a guy now. Did you beef yourself up?

Right now I'm about the size I was my senior year of high school football. I was a little shy of five foot ten, and I weighed one hundred and eighty—five pounds. Later, when I got to Marshall [University in West Virginia on a football scholarship], they wanted me to be an outside linebacker. I beefed up. I weighed like two twenty. My legs were gigantic; I was a beast.

(Shakes his head and grimaces.) Gosh, I was twenty . . . nineteen to twenty-one. You know, football was great, but I realized that it wasn't the same anymore. I didn't finish playing at Marshall. At that level it was such a business. I didn't like the philosophy, I didn't like the attitude. I played with some great people, and I made some good friends, but I didn't agree with the methods. I thought I shouldn't be squandering the rest of my two years at Marshall, giving my life to football and these coaches when I could be doing something better. And that was: Start hitting the books; start studying. Grow up and do something that's going to benefit you in the future. That's when I started applying myself academically and getting good grades and was able to get into law school. I gave up football. I'd started at eight. I loved the game. But it was time to move on.

So you went to law school in Chicago, then what?

(George turns solemn, stares into the air above my head). I worked for a Chicago law firm in a tall building, but didn't like it. I could not see myself living in that kind of environment every day. I wanted to come back, be closer to my family. I love Vermont. I love the beauty. There's no

place like it. I wanted to be a trial lawyer. (Shakes his head, grimaces.) Trial lawyers are almost extinct today. Cases don't go to trial. I had been interviewed with other firms before I came here and I got funny looks almost. I got discouraged. But when I came to this firm and met Bill Clausen and we talked for the first time, I told him, "Ya know, I'm kind of discouraged. I want to be a trial lawyer and I'm hearing nobody tries cases anymore; it's a thing of the past." He said, "Not with me, it isn't."

My first case for the firm was a major felony trial involving a guy whose brother I went to school with at Hanover High. His family came into the office and said, "We want you to represent him." I said, "I'm brand new; you need somebody with more experience." They said, "No, we know you, George. We want you." I was just licensed. I mean it was my first jury trial. It was huge stakes. He was charged with three felonies and a DWI [Driving While Intoxicated]. After the trial, I was drained; I was practically crying. I thought I'd let him down, I thought I did a terrible job. Before the verdict I thought I didn't know what I was doing . . . why did I agree to do this felony case? I said to myself, "I'm terrible, I shouldn't have done this." The jury came back, "Not guilty." What a way to start! I felt so emotionally drained; it was unbelievable. It was an amazing weight off my shoulders.

Now that you're a successful trial lawyer, how do you like it?

(Fingers together, he thinks a few moments.) I always considered myself sort of a fighter. A gladiator. That's why I liked football so much. I fell in love with football because to me it was like the only place you can still strap on armor, like the old warriors, and go do battle. You're putting everything in your heart and your soul into it. That's how I approached the game. That's sort of what I think's inside me. And I thought, Man, maybe being a trial lawyer I could use that kind of strength and passion. You're a warrior still, but you're channeling it in a different direction. Instead of using swords and being on a horse, or fighting on a field, you're fighting in a courtroom, which is the new field. These are just the kinds of ideas that I had, and I thought this might be a great way to do it, and if I could make a living doing it, even better.

I've become very busy. I've been here ten years and last year was one of my best.

So, it's almost time for the trial . . . what do you do? How do you get centered, all your information in order?

My last week's routine is just dress rehearsal. This is my philosophy: You need to be prepared to deliver the case a month before you're actually before the jury. My preparation is done well in advance of the trial. If I'm not just reviewing and polishing up during the last week, there is something wrong. My last few days, what I'm doing is staying pretty much to myself. I'm not doing anything big socially. I relax. I practice my opening statement, my closing argument. I say them out loud, to hear the words. I just listen to myself; I don't do it in front of a mirror. I just envision the jury sitting there and I'm talking to the jury. But you need to hear the words, how they sound when they come out of your mouth. It's one thing to write it down, but I think you need to hear the words that you're going to say.

(He laughs, leans back, fingers intertwined.) I find I'm way over prepared. Not in a bad way. When I'm in the trial, when I come out, I think, Wow, I was so well prepared for that; I probably didn't need to do that extra forty hours that I did, but I wouldn't do it any other way.

During a trial do you speak to the jury individually? How do you act?

It's very important that you be real. Be who you are. Be straight and honest with the jury. I've seen lawyers and their eyes quickly span back and forth across the whole jury. There's no connection. When I'm in front of a jury, the most important thing for me to let them know is that I really care about my client and my case. If you don't care about your client and your case, you can't win. You *have* to care. If you don't care, why should they care? So I don't treat them all like a single group. I make connections with individuals when I'm talking to a jury, just like I'm talking to friends. I convey my case. I hope I have a good case . . . an honest case . . . a just case. I show that I care.

Do you consider yourself more of an emotional, physical, or intellectual man?

I'm definitely more emotional. In my job, my cases; in my personal life, definitely more emotional. And there are a lot of emotions. In this line of work, love is the most powerful. I think it's probably the most powerful, no matter what you do. I don't mean to sound mushy saying that, but if I'm going to a lawyer or a doctor, I want to know I'm seeing somebody who loves his work, loves his client. Will do anything for him. I've heard too many lawyers say, "Be unemotional. Don't get involved with your clients." I'm not like that.

So you prefer a jury if you're trying to right an injustice?

Most certainly. You can't get justice from a corporation, from an insurance company, or a judge always . . . they won't give it to you. But a jury from a community of regular people who honestly care about you, they will listen, they will see it. The jury is the great equalizer of justice. They're the ones who, in my estimation, are truly detached from the big politics, from favoring any agency or organization. A judge may be more inclined to decide [a case] based on his personal background. But the jury—you've got twelve people from the community who have *the* most power at the end of the day. They don't have to answer to no one. You cannot interrogate them; they do not have to give you a rationale for why they did what they did. When it's David and Goliath, when it's the big money against the poor guy, when it's unfair attorneys or judges who are out to get you, the jury are your friends. That's it. A just result will come.

You can't trust justice to a judge or a police officer . . . or to a single person . . . or to someone working for the government or with connections or allegiances to some group. A jury that comes in blind and blank, they're the ones, the equalizer.

Why is it so difficult nowadays to get a jury trial if it's the most just?

Big money benefits from prolonging a case. Insurance companies slow down the legal process, stretch it out, delay things. The status quo is foot dragging. The rules and procedural paperwork are unreal. The strategy means it takes longer for a person to get justice. Family law is awful; everybody has a hand out and is getting paid. Mediation (shakes his head) is a waste of time. The emphasis is to resolve the case before a trial. Justice is less well served than finance. The legal maneuvers now make the money, just like the procedures in medicine. Lawyers forget their clients.

I need to ask you my classic Vermont questions: You ever milk a cow?

I've milked goats. My family used to have goats when we moved up here. We would milk the goats and try to make feta. (He chuckles.) All I can remember is things hanging and you're straining.

Ever make maple syrup?

No.

Ever can food?

I have friends who do it. They don't go to the grocery store, but they're older, retired. They can spend their time and energy doing that. I love going there for dinner because they go down in the basement where it's cool, and they pick out the chicken, the beef, the deer, or the moose. Vegetables? Shelves of them. I think it's awesome. I'd love to garden, raise my own food. I'd love to grow my own vegetables. I'd love to tap trees for syrup. I'd love to do all that kind of stuff. But I can't do that *and* work six days a week as a lawyer.

Do you hunt?

Yeah, I hunt. I hunt birds in New Hampshire. I have a .30-06, a .30-30. I have a 16-gauge shotgun. A .38 special pistol.

Do you have a license to carry a firearm?

In Vermont you don't need a license.

You practice here in the Upper Valley; what percent of cases are in Vermont and what percent in New Hampshire?

I'd say it's about fifty-fifty.

How many times do you face a jury in a year?

Three or four times a year. But most of my cases are civil; you're talking about money, not liberty. My last big cases were in Orange County, in the Chelsea courthouse. One was a sibling dispute over the father's will. The other was a land dispute between neighbors. Both will probably go to the Vermont Supreme Court.

What's been your biggest case?

A mentally-ill guy named Joseph Fortunati. A SWAT team went up in the woods and shot him. He was camping at the end of a public trail that looked like a rough logging road, right next to his father's property. Environmental workers were in the area, trying to locate an old copper mine. They stumbled across Joseph's camp site. They asked Joseph to move his tent out of the way because they wanted to drive through there. Joseph said, "No, you're on private property; this is where I live. And you guys are lost anyway." They reported him to the State Police. The State Police knew who Joseph was; they knew he had a history of mental illness. He had some problems with the police before. Never violent. They decided, instead of sending regular troopers, to send in a SWAT team to take him into custody. They ended up killing him. In my opinion unjustifiably. The federal judge has dismissed my lawsuit. We're in the process of filing an appeal to the Second Court of Appeals in Manhattan and having our day in front of a jury.

In your experience in Vermont, do judges usually defend law enforcement people?

Yes. I think there are some good judges out there, there are some that aren't so good. But they all work for the government. It doesn't take me to say it; this is what other people say. If it's my word against a cop's word, isn't the judge going to believe the cop? Mostly that's true. Not always, but mostly.

The judges work for the state, the prosecutors work for the state, the police work for the state. You've got to be seen as a judge tough on crime. You can't be a weak judge. (George leans across the desk and raises his voice.) You can't be a weak judge! So people laugh at you. You can't be known as the judge who goes against the cops or doesn't give them a little bit of favoritism without bending the law too much. You just can't. It's too political. I've seen that often. Not always. The good ones don't do that. But I've seen it often.

What about the future in Vermont? What would you like to see happen?

I wish it wasn't so hard for people to find justice. It's getting more difficult to use the court system to get it for people. There are many times I have a case where clients aren't guilty of the crimes charged, from a DUI [Driving Under the Influence] to a serious felony case, but they eventually take a deal. Plead guilty to something lesser [than they were charged]. Pay a small fine. Don't go to jail. But still plead guilty to something under the law that they're not guilty of because they can't afford to go to court and spend all this time and post bond and bail. So on and so forth. Economically, it's hard for people, and I wish that would change.

Culturally, what do you do? You like music, you read?

I certainly love women. I play the piano. I like live music. Sometimes I drive to Burlington to Higher Ground. Last time was to see Grace Potter.

Books? I'm a trial lawyer junky. I read histories of lawyers. I've read Plato on Socrates three or four times. Socrates was one of my heroes. To me, he was a trial lawyer. He always presented his position, and through rational thought and logic and argument, he presented his case. Here was a brilliant, brilliant man who never claimed to be brilliant. So smart. Intellectually powerful but very, very humble. Walked around with beat-up sandals and, I think, the same clothing. He was not beautiful in appearance. He never charged a fee. He just went out into the public and anybody who wanted to listen could listen. There was no one better. And when he had his trial, he spoke the truth. He was straight. He was principled about it. He didn't care what the consequences would be. And he was brilliant. I love reading about him.

What about social media?

Progress is great, but I have refused as much as I could, even being a lawyer, to get caught up in the technology boom. I don't have a cell phone. I don't have an iPod or whatever they're called . . . Blackberries . . . and these sorts of things. So, you say, "You need those things to function these days." That's true, but it's gone to such an extent . . . we've gotten fat on stuff. We're all just sort of complacent about it. And I don't like it.

If you were to summarize the last decade of George Spaneas, trial lawyer, how would you describe it?

I hope I've been fair, decent, and honest to people. And helped them out. I hope in the last ten years that I've done good things for people. But maybe the answer is still out there. ∎

Sometimes you just have to cry

Sara Stark

Born: December 31, 1976
Where: Essex Junction, VT
Siblings: one brother, older; one sister, older
College: Castleton State College
Degree: Art, Special Education graduate degree
Married: Yes, three kids
Job: Special Educator

> Sara Stark lives in an eye-catching Victorian house along Route 4A in
> Hydeville, a section of Castleton, a college town close to the New York
> border. The house was empty for ten years when Sara and her husband
> Josh bought it back in 1998. They spent the next decade restoring the
> house, adding a coach barn that doubles as a garage. The house is a
> visual knock-out: seafoam green, with purple, blue, yellow, and white
> trim. Inside, I find Sara with her three young boys in the kitchen. After
> introductions and a brief tour of the ground floor, Josh leads the boys
> upstairs. At the base of the stairs, in an immaculate dining room with
> antique furniture, Sara and I sit and talk about the challenging realities
> of her life beneath the deceptively tranquil surface: being a special ed
> teacher in tough times and having an autistic son at home and worrying
> about her husband, a plumber, now laid off.

So it sounds like you've been impacted by the economy.

We've been significantly impacted. Josh has been unemployed since late
last year and the state can't afford to send kids to residential placements. I
work for a private school, Camp E-Wen-Akee in Benson. It has gone from
a capacity of thirty kids down to fifteen. We did take both boys and girls,
but the numbers have been down lately so we closed our girls' group. Now
there are no programs for girls. It's not that there are no girls in the state
who are in need; it's a financial issue.

Where do the students come from?

Usually, they're mental-health referrals. It's a therapeutic, wilderness,
residential program; the students are in custody. Counselors live with the
students in the woods. They go on canoe trips, they go backpacking, they
build structures. They've had struggles with substance abuse, run-ins with
the law, family problems. The program [helps them] learn coping skills so

they can be available for learning. I provide them with learning opportunities; it depends if they're available. I take every opportunity to get some teaching in.

Do you find the work a real challenge?

Yeah. I've been here five years. The unique thing is that I worked in public schools before coming into this program. I had a very different perspective. I had a difficult time transitioning from public school. Now I understand that the great majority of the kids have experienced so much abuse, a lot of them, so many difficulties and real life trauma, that they need to confront those before they can focus on other things. Not that learning doesn't take place, but it's just so different from public school . . . there's a lot more going on.

Do you fear that the economy is going to sweep your whole school away?

I have wondered that, actually. When I started there, there were three teachers and myself. And I was only part time. We had less and less students, budget issues. As people left—they had a baby or other reasons— we didn't hire those positions back. So right now there's just one other teacher . . . and myself. And the director, an education coordinator. We're still getting revenue in, so there's no fear of closing down. The other thing, in Vermont there are not a lot of placement options. So many programs are full.

Beyond school, and your family, who makes up your community? Do you have a lot of friends here?

We don't have a lot of friends. We've kind of somewhat isolated ourselves by working on our house every weekend for the last ten years. I mean, we bought our house when I was twenty-one. While our friends were off having fun, we were working. I think that now our kids are starting to get into school, we're starting to meet some more people, which is nice.

What would you like to see that might improve the area?

Having three young kids, having something to do—I mean, I'm from Essex Junction, which was not a big town but there was always a strong rec program. I think they're trying to get that going . . . but it's not here yet. That's one thing. The other thing is . . . you know, my middle son is autistic. [I'd like to have] more here to do with autistic kids. (Sara hesitates, searches for the right words.) Vermont doesn't have a whole lot to offer. Just more therapies and more specialists, that would be helpful.

How do you handle the situation with your son?

How do I handle it? (Blank faced, she thinks a moment.) The way I took it at first was as a special educator—you don't know anything [about something like this] when it comes to your own child. Probably, if you were a doctor, it'd be the same thing. When emotion's tied to the issue, it's out the door.

For services now he does go to Triple E [Early Essential Education] at the Castleton Elementary School. It's like a model program where they supposedly mix half students with special needs and half a model peer group that they can learn from. So he goes there four mornings a week. Then he goes to a place in Rutland called Kids on the Move that provides services. He goes to a swimming therapy and occupational therapy. My parents come down to help; I don't want to leave him with just anybody. They come down and stay overnight two nights a week so I can go to work.

What triggers autism? Do they know or is it still pretty much a mystery?

A lot of people think it's related to the mercury in vaccines. The newest number I just read was one in ninety-one children [are autistic]; the number has gone up significantly. Because autism is such a spectrum, they're identifying a lot of high-functioning autism, or Asperger's, whereas in the past they might have just been [seen as] a little different or [having] some quirky-type behavior. Now they're labeling it.

Sara Stark ◆ 203

Some say there's a connection between diet and autism characteristics. I've been reading about gluten-free, casein-free diets. So this week Wyatt started a gluten-dairy-egg-soy-free diet. He only eats a very limited number of foods. So I've been making my own chicken nuggets and French fries. All this is time consuming, trying to do it.

Do you suspect a vaccine in your situation?

I don't. Some people say their child was developing fine, then after a vaccine they got very sick. Then their child was gone. Some people think there's maybe a genetic component. With Wyatt, in utero, he never moved. I just remember—and he's my second—I just remember saying, "He's never moving." When he was born, he slept; I couldn't even wake him up to feed him. They all said (she adopts a happy voice), "Well, kids are all different." It was from the beginning with him.

When you decompress, let off steam, what do you do?

I talk. I do have an elliptical machine; it's quite new. But I mostly talk.

Is your husband a good listener?

No. (She laughs.) Yeah, sometimes . . . if there are no other distractions around—three little kids tugging at his pants leg. Yeah, I do talk to him. I do use my elliptical; it's supposed to take the pressure off your knees compared to a treadmill. You didn't go upstairs; we have a little gym up there.

Do you consider yourself primarily a physical, emotional or intellectual person?

Emotional . . . yeah, emotional.

What's your ethnic background? What do your parents do?

French? (Said almost as a question.) My father was a systems analyst at IBM. My emotional side probably comes from my mom. She was in human resources [for ski companies and then for Jog Bra]. These companies were all in Vermont, but then they moved out. It was like a joke: whichever company she worked for, they moved out of the state.

In high school I liked sports, and boys. I played track. Shot put and discus; they were in the family. My sister did them, my grandfather. I didn't start doing art until college.

When you studied art, did you study much art history?

I did. But don't quiz me on any of it. I don't follow the Vermont art scene; I wish I did. In the garage, we're rebuilding the upstairs right now and half of it will be my studio space. Where I can hide out. (She smiles.)

I can't wait! I haven't painted or drawn or sewn . . . I haven't done any of that. So we're hoping we can get that done and I can have a room.

If you were being interviewed for a new job and were asked to briefly sum up your experience over the last decade, what would you say?

(A long pause.) Hmmm . . . hopefully, I wouldn't give them that blank stare. You know, it's hard not to roll the whole parenting piece into it. I think about kids a lot. I think about kids all the time. About being hard working and patient, about being the best advocate that I can for them as a parent and a teacher. I'd roll into that that I tend to be creative . . . (she smiles fleetingly) . . . and sometimes I wonder if I should have gone into a different field.

In the last ten years again, what was your high point, the best time? And your low point, when you kind of bottomed out?

Having kids is probably both answers. Taking on this house is one of the most rewarding things I've ever done because, you know, we did all the work ourselves. I'm kind of a life-long learner, happy I finished college and finished grad school. I just actually finished an autism certificate program.

Has having an autistic child made you grow in unique ways?

Definitely . . . definitely. I think having a child with spectrum is bitter sweet. That's definitely the low point. I'll not cry . . . . No, I may cry. (Tries to laugh as she wipes her tears.)

I'm a parent, and you always feel guilty yourself: What did I do? What did I cause? How come this happens to me? But then it has some real beauty to it because it makes you into a bigger human.

Yeah . . . not necessarily stronger. (She laughs and swipes her eyes.)

Between you and me I don't think we need stronger people; we need more compassionate people.

For myself, realizing how many stereotypes are out there about autism, I think that was a big one. People tend to have a bad idea of what autistic kids look like, and how they act. That's not accurate.

Down point? I couldn't say it before, but when we left the doctor's one time, they said, "There's a good chance he'll never live on his own." (The tears flow.) I don't know why I'm crying. Part of me now looks back—you don't want to hear that about your kid at any age. Boy, someone having the balls to say that your kid at three will never live on his own. How can they say that? At first, it was the shock of, "Wow!" Then, "How dare you?" So then you try to do everything to try to prove they're wrong.

What about your future? Where would you like to see yourself in ten years?
There are so many things I want to do. There really are. I'd like to get involved with the town, in some capacity. I'd like to start up a support group for parents; I think so often kids are diagnosed with whatever, and then it's like, "See ya later," and they're sent out the door. There's a lot of support that families need during that time that they don't necessarily get.

Part of me feels that I'd like to go back to public school. My job [at Camp E-Wen-Akee] works for me . . . it's part time. But it's so different from public school; it's year round and there's no vacations. We don't get benefits. But the other part of me thinks because I'm so consumed with kids—you kind of lose yourself—I'd like to have time just to paint and do my own thing.

What direction would you like to see the state taking?
I'd like to see them stop cutting budgets. There's one program that helps identify kids with special needs before they're Triple E age. Before the age of three. They're cutting its budget, they're cutting respite care. There are budget cuts everywhere. I'd like that to stop.

Where would the money come from? You have any visions about how the revenue stream might increase, since state budgets are mostly tax funded?
(Talking sort of to herself.) How to increase revenue? Working more on increasing tourism? Getting people visiting? We do have a lot to offer, with skiing, as long as the weather cooperates. I don't know.

Okay, let's shift to my classic Vermont questions: You ever milk a cow?
No . . . I hate cows. (Laughs.) I think they're the ugliest . . . from a distance they look nice, but closer they're all bony and gross looking.

How about tapping maple trees?
I've done that. Actually, at our school, that's part of our program. The kids tap trees and we have a sugar house. They make it, and they each get to bring a quart home.

How about canning or putting food by?
Yeah, I love to can. My grandmother always used to can. (Sara's boys are calling for her from upstairs.) She used to can everything. We had a big garden and we did tomatoes. She was a teacher but she also sewed [her six kids'] clothes. She lived through the Depression, and she didn't spend any money for anything. I spent a lot of time with her, making jams and jellies. Canned all the vegetables. ("Mom!" comes floating down the stairs.) For me, there's nothing more rewarding. For one, you know you did all the

work, and you know what is in your food. Then to be able to grow it. Then all the money you're saving by not buying.

Are you a hunter?

My family are hunters and fishermen. I used to want to get my own hunting license. I never did. All of my boys have theirs; you can buy them the first year, a lifetime hunting and fishing license. So they're all set to go. But I grew up ice fishing a lot. My brother and brother-in-law [love ice fishing.] My grandmother, who did all the canning, she was *the* ice fisherman. Down here my brother put on an ice-fishing derby on Lake Dunmore. Josh brought our older boy out there.

Culturally, are you a movie fan, read a lot, like music?

I like music. I used to be all classic rock. Enjoyed that. Now I turn the radio on, and Josh says I fit into what all the thirteen-year-olds like on the radio. On my MP3 is what's on the radio; it's good to work out to. I like movies, Netflix. I read; I'm reading a lot on autism.

Social media: do you use it much?

Yes, to connect with friends and family. My work does have a page.

Do you have a favorite quote?

I'll think about it. It's how I process things: I'll think of it in a couple of hours.

(Later, Sara sends me an email.) I don't have a favorite quote, but I do have a favorite poem, "Welcome to Holland." You can find it on the Web. ∎

Acknowledgments

The idea for this book may have fallen out of the sky, but it wouldn't have gone far on the ground without the help of other people. Steering us to the twenty young Vermonters in these pages were Tosca Smith, Morgan Daybell, Beth Crane, Dennis Tatro, Rolf Anderson, Stu McGowan, Jim Schley, Shirley Reid, Tim Matson, Kathy Ross, Geof Hewitt, and Louis Dandurand. Sandra Beatty and Laura Tatro provided graphics and photography guidance; Laura's husband Dennis was our web designer. Richard Cowperthwait and Chris O'Shea talked to us about the first decade of the new millennium in detail, only to have their words end up on the cutting-room floor. For that we apologize. A very special thanks goes to Jim Schley for his enthusiastic support of the project from its inception, guidance at various stages, and wisdom about virtually all aspects of publishing, whether it be print or ebooks. Alice Fogel did the editing, finding narrative lines where we didn't know they existed, vastly improving the text, and then steering us to Sid Hall, book designer and print guru extraordinaire. Last but not least, Viola Woodward did our proofreading.

To all of you, a great big thanks.

About the Author and Photographer

JOE SHERMAN is a writer of international acclaim. *Fast Lane on a Dirt Road: A Contemporary History of Vermont* is a classic of regional history. *In the Rings of Saturn* was nominated for a Pulitzer Prize for nonfiction. His work set in Central Europe recently appeared in the anthology: *The Return of Kral Majales: Prague's International Literary Renaissance 1990-2010*. He has received two Fulbright Foundation specialist awards. Shorter work has appeared in many magazines, including *Smithsonian, Audubon, Yankee, The New England Review, Automobile, Vermont Life,* and *The Prague Literary Review. Young Vermonters: Not An Endangered Species* is his first book of interviews. He lives in northern Vermont.

MARTINA TESAŘOVÁ lives in Vermont and Prague, Czech Republic. She is a translator and photographer.

A word from the photographer: These photographs were made quickly without too much preparation or control. I didn't aspire to get artsy. I wanted straightforward documentary-like photos that caught the personalities of the people, the atmosphere of the interviews and  their settings. The idea was to get mug shot quality portraits and then, during the interview, more relaxed snapshots. The photos were taken on the spot where each interview took place, usually in homes and workplaces. I had to improvise with given light conditions and settings. It was fun, and a challenge.

All photos were shot with a Cannon G10. For mug shots I used a background reflector, a white background board and a main light behind my camera. For most snapshots, I steered clear from using the flash because it was a distracting element. My photographs have been professionally published (including *Automobile,* and *The Return of Kral Majales: Prague's International Literary Renaissance 1990-2010*). This is my first book.